SARA BLAU

CLOSE *to You*

DAILY SPIRITUAL MOTIVATION

Inspired by the Tanya

Close to You:
Daily Spiritual Motivation
Inspired by the Tanya

Second Edition — 2022

Published by Meaningful Life Center

ISBN: 978-1-8865-8701-4

Written by Sara Blau
Design by Batsheva Lubin

Meaningful Life Center
788 Eastern Parkway, Suite 303
Brooklyn, NY 11213-3409
(718) 774-6448
For more information, visit www.meaningfullife.com or call (800) 3–MEANING.

NOTE FROM THE AUTHOR

Life in the 21st century could be hectic. It could be a kaleidoscope of flashing images and technology, with multiple responsibilities vying for our attention. And as life swirls around us in blinding color, we sometimes crave that calm, grounding center: something to hold onto so that everything else could settle. We search for a piece of sanity, a spiritual anchor.

The holy book of Tanya is such a source. It is a book of deep spiritual concepts, yet written for the average Jew. It is based on a verse in Deuteronomy 30:14: "No, the thing is very close to you, in your mouth and in your heart, to observe it...." *Close to You* is literally the point of the Tanya, and the actual point of this volume you are holding in your hand. What better way to provide a center for the modern Jewish woman than with a book of short bursts of inspiration: nuggets that can inspire you and motivate you to serve G-d according to your capacity; a book to invite you to delve deeper whenever you have the chance; a book to show you that *it is close to you* to serve G-d whoever you are, wherever you are?

Serving G-d is relevant. Serving G-d is realistic. And here is a manual to show you, in bite-sized nuggets, just how.

Just like a well-rounded meal has an appetizer, a main course, and a dessert, each piece in this book has a hook, an expounded idea, and a takeaway dessert for you to keep chewing on—a line that you can take with you, sweet as chocolate pudding, to inspire the rest of your day. That can help you get unstuck emotionally and spiritually, and keep you focused during the day.

So if you've never studied Tanya, this book is for you.

If you've studied Tanya just a bit but felt it was out of your league, this is for you. And if you've studied the Tanya but are at a loss how to apply its teachings to everyday life, this is for you.

Use this book as a springboard for meditation. Journal about it. Internalize the one-liners that can accompany you throughout your day, proving to you that it is indeed *close to you* to serve G-d with true love and awe.

Sara Blau

TABLE OF CONTENTS

REALISTIC EXPECTATIONS

THE PREMISE OF THE TANYA: "CLOSE TO YOU"

Have you seen a cooking show lately: the type with show-stopping desserts and 10-course meals that can be completed in 60 minutes? You know, all you need are some "essential tools" and about 15 hours of prep time. But don't worry, it's perfectly attainable for even the most inexperienced in the kitchen.

It's a tease, and it makes me revert to being a teenager, saying, "Right," with a mental eyeball roll.

We like it when expectations are realistic—when things seem accessible. And we often feel so helpless when they are not.

This is the theme of the book of Tanya. In the Torah, G-d tells the Jews that keeping the *mitzvot* is not out of reach. "Rather, [this] thing is very close to you; it is in your mouth and in your heart, so that you can fulfill it" *(Deuteronomy 30:14).*

We desperately want to feel that way, but what tools do we have at our disposal? How is it so "close"?

The 53 chapters of Tanya have some answers. And learning Tanya makes it clear that within every Jew lies the ability to be a *beinoni*, the hero of the Tanya.

(Inspired by the title page of Tanya)

TANYA BIT: G-d has realistic and "age-appropriate" expectations of me. Fulfilling His commandments is within my reach.

GET TO KNOW YOU

CHAPTERS 1—8

Are you the best of the best or the worst of the worst? You feel capable of both—because you have two forces inside you. The Tanya removes the shock factor by giving you a glimpse and vocabulary to name the two opposing forces within you: a G-dly soul and an animal soul. Each soul can be expressed in thought, speech, and action, and you have the ability to switch from one extreme to the other. What drives the two souls?

A SURPRISING OATH

FROM BEFORE YOU WERE BORN

What is your earliest memory? Were you three? Four? None of us remember
when we were babies, never mind before we were born. Yet the soul has an
entire history before it even descends to this world.

The Tanya opens with a surprising oath administered to every Jewish soul before it descends to
this world: "Be righteous and be not wicked; and even if the whole world tells you that you are
righteous, regard yourself as wicked."

Now, this could go in two directions. A person could take a psychological hit, and be depressed at
the thought that no matter what he does he will always be wicked. However, feeling so inadequate
is hardly conducive to serving G-d joyfully.

Or, a person can be resigned to failure and "wicked" status, and make a firm resolution not to let
it bother him. But how can one work to refrain from sin while simultaneously not caring that he
is wicked?

There must be some nuance that we're missing here, an interpretation that would shed light on the
cryptic oath. That's the definition we're after, and the one that the Tanya will provide.

(Inspired by Chapter 1 of Tanya)

 TANYA BIT: Both depression and indifference at my spiritual state can interfere with
my service of G-d.

RELATIVE STATUS?

OR OBJECTIVE DEFINITIONS?

Ever heard the phrase "It's all relative"? It's true: many descriptions in life are accurate only relative to something else being described. A color might be considered "cool" relative to one color, and "warm" relative to another. A house might be called "large" compared to an apartment and would be "tiny" compared to a mansion. But if you start calling the mansion "tiny," where does that leave the studio apartment?...

The Gemara talks about five categories of people. A complete and an incomplete *tzaddik* (righteous person); a complete and an incomplete *rasha* (wicked person); and the intermediate guy, the *beinoni*. Rabbah, a great man in his own right, once declared, "I, for example, am a *beinoni*." His disciple Abbaye responded, "If *you*, who learns Torah day and night, are just a '*beinoni*'—the intermediate, average man—then where does that leave the rest of society?!"

Clearly, Webster's dictionary does not suffice to explain the true definition for righteous, wicked, and intermediate. And to indicate that even further, we read of Job's complaint to G-d: "L-rd of the Universe! You have created righteous men, You have created wicked men...." He did not intend to remove free choice from humanity, so what does it mean that G-d creates righteous and wicked?

Journey on as the Tanya elaborates on an objective definition of the above terms, by getting to the core of what makes up the psyche of a Jew.

(Inspired by Chapter 1 of Tanya)

 TANYA BIT: The level of a *beinoni* is far deeper than just a 50-percent Jew. And yet you and I can reach that level.

A PERPETUAL PARADOX

THE TWO SOULS WITHIN

It's like there are two people living inside of me. I feel the need to be altruistic, coupled with the need for self-preservation. I feel my heart bleed for the poor, but can't bear to part with too much hard-earned money. I have all the intentions of being a loving, patient spouse and parent; I feel indignant, provoked, and just want my own space. Who am I?

Ready for the bombshell? There really are two forces inside of me. The contradictions swirling around do not make me a hypocrite, but they are the inevitable result of the way G-d created me. As it says about every Jew: "And *neshamot* [souls] which I have made" *(Isaiah 57:16)*. This means that in every one of us are two opposing drives, each with its own set of desires.

One is called the "animal soul," the natural instinctive life force that runs in our bloodstream. Like an animal, this drive is focused on the survival of self, considering only its own immediate needs. The other is the "G-dly soul," which drives the desire to cling to G-d and fulfill His commandments.

An eternal game of tug of war, indeed.

(Inspired by Chapter 1 of Tanya)

 TANYA BIT: The fact that I struggle is not because I am a hypocrite, but because I have two souls trying to assert themselves.

WHAT'S YOUR ELEMENT?

THE ANIMAL SOUL'S TENDENCIES

A popular pastime among my friends in high school was anything that had to do with self-analyzing. Handwriting analysis, picture analysis, or personality analysis—as long as it helped bring self-awareness, it was cool.

The Tanya introduces us to a new form of personality—one not in the books we were reading—and it had to do with four elements. All matter can be classified into fire, air, water, and earth (this was much easier than the elements in chemistry class!), and each of the four elements spiritually symbolizes a core character trait of the animal soul. The animal soul is not evil but may present negative characteristics in its quest to cater to its own selfish or instinctive needs.

Fire:

Anger erupts like a raging fire, rising and destroying. Fire represents the personality of one who is easily vexed and whose pride is easily punctured.

Water:

Water is indispensable for the growth of many of life's pleasures, such as delectable foods of both the plant and animal varieties. Water, therefore, represents the personality of one who has an insatiable appetite for life's material pleasures and is constantly on the lookout for more.

Air:

Air has no meaningful substance; it represents the personality of one who enjoys empty talk or boasting.

Earth:

Earth represents depression and laziness, as one who is depressed is drawn downward in an earthlike fashion. This personality feels a heaviness and a lack of motivation to get things done.

What every animal soul has in common is the drive to satisfy physical needs and desires.

However, each of our animal souls has a unique combination of the above four elements, giving us a unique set of challenges to tackle.

(Inspired by Chapter 1 of Tanya)

 TANYA BIT: I will consider which of the four elements resonates as my instinctive nature, and I will work to make improvements.

INFINITE WORTH

THE G-DLY SOUL

A healthy self-esteem is considered to be all the rage today, with a lack of it being
blamed for a myriad of problems and its presence a predictor of great success.
So what really is the secret to a strong self-esteem?

It's being aware of a deeper part of oneself, an infinite part: the G-dly soul that every Jew—from
the most righteous person to the biggest sinner—possesses. Every soul goes through a spiritual
process before entering the body, which affects its level, yet every Jew at his or her core has a
pure soul: a soul that was breathed into man by G-d himself, from deep within Him. For just as a
person's thought is more internal than his speech, the source of a Jew's soul is from a higher, more
internal level (G-d's thought) than the source of all other creations (G-d's speech).

What is the implication? That regardless of my performance or status, there is a completely
selfless, holy drive within me that wants to connect to G-d and fulfill His *mitzvot*. And even if I feel
like I've stumbled or failed, I can always remember that I have a part of me that is a treasure—a
literal piece of G-d Himself.

(Inspired by Chapter 2 of Tanya)

 TANYA BIT: I have a G-dly soul inside of me, with infinite value and inherent
goodness.

A FEELING IS BORN...

THE G-DLY SOUL'S THOUGHTS AND EMOTIONS

"YOU ARE MAKING ME MAD!" We sometimes want to yell that at the top of our lungs—whether at a child, neighbor, or that random person who cuts us off in traffic. In truth, however, do other people or situations actually cause our feelings? Or is it something internal that produces them?

The Alter Rebbe explains that our thought process and what we choose to focus on will dictate which feelings arise in our hearts. That means that our emotions are born not due to specific events, but due to how we process those events. The more we delve into a specific thought, the more those corresponding emotions will develop in our heart. If we focus on how unjust a situation is or how inconsiderate a person is, then we are sure to feel the anger and resentment building up.

So, what is the secret to feeling "holy" or G-dly feelings, such as love and awe of G-d? Allowing our G-dly soul to use its cognitive abilities to contemplate how great G-d is. These cognitive abilities include *chochmah*, which is the first flash of intuition or grasping a concept; *binah*, the ability to study and get a real understanding of a concept; and *da'as*, really focusing and meditating on a concept until it causes real emotional change. G-dly emotions are bound to form when one grasps, studies, and focuses on G-d's greatness: how He is literally the life force of every created being, and at the same time so much more transcendent. How small we are in comparison to Him, to the point where we are nothing at all. Meditating on these thoughts will naturally lead to feelings of awe and humility, as well as love towards a G-d who gives us life and sustenance on a daily basis.

It turns out that our intellectual abilities are the Mom and Dad of the desirable children: the emotions. *(Inspired by Chapter 3 of Tanya)*

 TANYA BIT: Into which thought am I delving, and to which emotion is that giving birth?

SPIRITUAL WARDROBE

THE G-DLY SOUL'S MODE OF EXPRESSION

Watching my baby sit and babble on the floor, his blue eyes shining in wonder
as he discovers the world using all his senses, my heart feels ready to explode
with the love I have for this fellow. I **think** about how adorable he is, I **tell** him
how crazy his Mama is over him, and I scoop him up with a **tangible** squeeze
so tight, you'd think I was squeezing out toothpaste from a half-empty dispenser.
Because that is how I express my love.

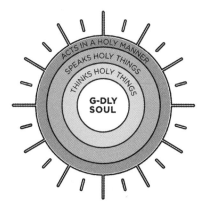

The G-dly soul, with its intellect and emotions, has similar modes of expression.

The G-dly soul **thinks** about holy things, using its intellectual powers to learn all the parts of
Torah, whether on the simplest level or the most esoteric. It **speaks** holy things, expressing its love
of G-d by speaking words of Torah, and it **acts** in a holy manner, by fulfilling the *mitzvot* of the
Torah. For it is love of G-d that drives the fulfillment of His commands, and the awe of G-d that
allows one to refrain from doing what is forbidden.

These three modes of expression are compared to "clothing" for the soul, for as any woman will tell you, clothing can be put on and off at will (just check out the pile as she gets ready for a party or *simchah*). Along similar lines, I may not be able to change the actual makeup of my soul, but thought, speech, and action can be freely "put on" and "put off," expressing the G-dly soul when I wish to. This concept lays the foundation for what will be defined as the category of the *beinoni*.

(Inspired by Chapter 4 of Tanya)

 TANYA BIT: My G-dly soul becomes visible when I "clothe" it with Torah and *mitzvot*.

A HOLY HUG

WHEN THE G-DLY SOUL DOES A MITZVAH

Can you imagine approaching G-d and hugging Him? Like, really embracing
His essence? Is such an encounter even possible?

In Chapter 4 of Tanya, the Alter Rebbe teaches us that it is. G-d, in all His greatness, humbly
enclothed Himself into this physical world and can be found in tangible things, such as in the ink
of the 24 books of Tanach and in the mundane items with which we perform *mitzvot*. When we—
regular flesh-and-blood people—learn a verse in Torah or perform a mitzvah, it's like we're giving
G-d a hug, connecting to the G-dliness found within physicality. Whether it's a coin for charity or
wine for kiddush, we tap into spirituality specifically through these objects.

In fact, this is the reason that one hour of human life on planet Earth spent performing good
deeds is more valuable than an everlasting afterlife in Heaven, for it is only through physicality
that one hugs the Essence of G-d. Physicality is not a distraction from holiness; it is the medium
through which every part of our being can connect to G-d on an intimate level.

It's true that we may not always feel that doing a mitzvah is hugging G-d, because the holiness
of the Torah is couched into such tangible, mundane terms that it feels like it is "covered up" by
layers of physicality. However, if you were hugging someone really special, would it matter how
many layers of clothing he or she was wearing? G-d may seem to be "wrapped" in all these layers,
but it's still Him that we're hugging.

(Inspired by Chapter 4 of Tanya)

 TANYA BIT: Doing a physical mitzvah is like giving G-d a hug.

DIGESTING G-D

WHEN THE G-DLY SOUL LEARNS TORAH

"But what's the point?!" We would grumble these words to our math teacher, wondering why we needed to spend endless hours understanding fractions and computing equations that we would never in our lives have to deal with, at least not without a calculator. So, what was the point of straining all those muscles in the brain?

Sometimes that was the point. Beyond getting educated, doing the math was meant to sharpen our brains and exercise higher-order thinking.

Learning Torah is far different from learning math. When one learns a piece of Torah that seems irrelevant, such as the Talmud discussing how much Reuven would owe Shimon in a hypothetical situation, it is not merely gym-for-the-brain. When one learns a *halachah* in Torah, the mind is internalizing G-d's will and wisdom, which is one with G-d. Not only is the subject matter enveloped by the mind, but the mind is enveloped and surrounded by the subject matter, in this case G-d's very wisdom. Mastering Torah means more than just digesting information, but digesting G-d Himself, so to speak, Who is otherwise not graspable by our very finite selves. Regardless of which law in Torah one studies, it is an opportunity for one to connect to the infinite G-d.

This is the advantage of Torah learning, even over performing *mitzvot*. We are not only embracing Him, as with all *mitzvot*, but we are "taking Him in," allowing Him into our very brains.

Torah is therefore called "food for the soul," for by grasping a concept in Torah, the soul is absorbing and "digesting" G-d. *(Inspired by Chapter 5 of Tanya)*

 TANYA BIT: By learning algebra, one doesn't unite with a triangle. But by learning Torah, one becomes unified with G-d.

EMOTIONAL IMMATURITY

THE ANIMAL SOUL'S THOUGHTS AND EMOTIONS

My toddler's ice cream fell on the floor.
Or his wobbly tower toppled over.
Or he didn't get the color he wanted.

In each of these cases, his response is swift and predictable, a full-blown tantrum
until he is comforted or distracted. His emotions easily overtake him, and what
seems insignificant to an adult can be the end of the world to a two-year-old.
His emotional maturity is in proportion to his intellectual ability, in this case an
underdeveloped brain which isn't able to put things in proportion.

Sometimes we are not that far off from toddlers. Though our temper tantrums don't necessarily
involve kicking and screaming, there are times when our emotions take over our thoughts, rather
than our thoughts initiating our emotions. While the G-dly soul focuses on holy thoughts that
will lead to wholesome and holy emotions, the animal soul's thoughts get carried away, fanning
the flames of its negative emotions. If the animal soul feels angry, its thoughts will continue to
ruminate about why it is justified in the anger, even fantasizing about revenge and hatred towards
the perpetrator.

In both cases, the intellect is the source for the emotions. But with the G-dly soul, the intellect is
in control. With the animal soul, the emotions reign supreme, like the instincts of a wild animal.

(Inspired by Chapter 6 of Tanya)

 TANYA BIT: Am I getting taken over by my emotions, or am I generating my
emotions?

THE "OTHER" WARDROBE

THE ANIMAL SOUL'S MODE OF EXPRESSION

Spring cleaning finds me knee-deep in piles of clothing, sorting through styles, sizes and seasons, trying to determine what's worth saving. Some goes to the basement, and some stays on the shelves; some become hand-me-downs, and some remain hopelessly outdated.

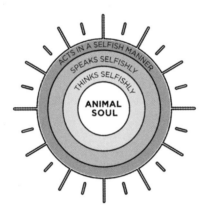

That's why clothing is such an apt metaphor for our thoughts, speech, and actions, as we are constantly evaluating which "clothing" to wear. The G-dly soul's "clothing" is generally easy to recognize, referring to living in sync with Torah: thinking thoughts of Torah, saying words of Torah, or doing an actual mitzvah. But what is the "clothing," or expressions of thought, speech, and action, of the animal soul? Does it express itself only as an evil devil? Hardly. The animal soul isn't evil, just selfish. In fact, 90 percent of our thoughts, speech, or actions can go either way, expressing the G-dly soul or the animal soul.

The difference is in the intention. Any mundane act under the sun—from eating to driving to reading on the couch—can be a selfish act, with no other intention than to satisfy my own personal craving. When I think, say or do something solely for my own selfish benefit or pleasure, I am expressing my animal soul. Yet the very same act can become transparent, in sync with the reason it was created, if it is intended for the service of G-d. For example, a muffin can be consumed gluttonously, or instead it can be consumed with purpose—not to satisfy a sweet tooth, but as fuel to be able to live, pray, and function as a Jewish woman.

Holiness happens when the ego of the animal soul is punctured, and I live my physical life not to gratify myself, but to have energy to do what G-d wants me to do.

(Inspired by Chapter 6 of Tanya)

 TANYA BIT: I can elevate the mundane with the power of intention.

PEELING THE FRUIT

REVEALING THE G-DLY SPARK IN PHYSICALITY

There are times when I feel like a peeler by profession. From bananas to oranges, from apples to eggs, I spend way too much time peeling foods for my little ones. It feels almost like a full-time job! The kids just can't wait to eat the good stuff.

Fruits and nuts aren't the only things with a shell that has to be removed.

Much of reality is covered in a shell, a layer that conceals the G-dliness found in the world. For instance, when a succulent piece of meat sizzling on a barbecue is paired with a crisp red wine, this seems to shout out corporeal pleasure, appearing to lack any holy purpose. But peeling the shell would mean revealing the truth—that a good wine and a satisfying meal can be the impetus for concentrating on a deep Torah class. When a person is hungry or distracted, his or her chances of concentration are low. Eating a delicious meal makes it possible to be present to learn.

There are other "prerequisites" to learning. As the great sage Rava once said: "Wine and fragrance make my mind more receptive." He did what it took to relax his brain—by drinking a glass of wine—to prepare himself to delve deep into learning Torah.

Cracking a good joke also does not appear to be holy in any way. Yet this same great Rava used to begin every Torah class with some humor, to open the hearts and minds of his students. A bad mood is hardly conducive to learning; he knew that laughter would relax their minds and allow his students to be more receptive to his teachings. In so many ways, Rava "peeled the shell off the fruit."

The Hebrew word for "shell" (including the ones that "hide" G-dliness) is *kelipah*. However, within *kelipah* there are two categories.

The first type is *kelipat nogah*, the *kelipah* with a little light inside it. Using some creativity, most things in the world can be utilized for a higher purpose by peeling away the shell to reveal the inner hidden potential (think steaks and jokes). Instead of expressing the animal soul, it can suddenly be a beautiful expression of the G-dly soul's desires.

But then there are things that are off-limits, declared by Torah unfit to be used in the service of G-d. An example for this category of *kelipah* is a nonkosher food, which cannot be eaten as a source of energy, even to accomplish great things. Acts forbidden by the Torah can never be "peeled." They can never express the G-dly soul.

So yes, it's a full-time job—this "peeling"—being conscious of how I can use the physical world to enhance my spiritual service, at the same time rejecting that which is not allowed according to Torah.

(Inspired by Chapter 7 of Tanya)

 TANYA BIT: Peeling the layers of physical existence reveals that we can be serving G-d around the clock, and not just in the synagogue.

THE POWER OF REVERSE
WHEN YOU TEMPORARILY FORGET ABOUT YOUR G-DLY SOUL

Sometimes it just happens. You go through the motions of your day, hardly aware of what you are doing, never mind why you are doing it. Or you space out, forgetting that with each physical act that you do, you can channel it into serving G-d. And so you engage in a mundane behavior without being super-mindful about intending to serve G-d with it. (This can desensitize you and lead to the next step.) Even worse, you eat or do something forbidden by the Torah, which lowers the act into the clutches of the lower level of *kelipah*, the impure spiritual forces in the universe.

Is there any way to reverse it?

There is. As soon as you discover that you have derailed—and decide to get back on track serving G-d with every physical act—you can retroactively insert a holy intention into any permissible action done without the express intention of serving G-d. So, suppose you may have been eating or exercising or working without being conscious of how this was all in order to serve G-d. As soon as you shift back into focus and actually use the energy you gained from such acts to pray, learn Torah, or perform any good deed, you can elevate that into holiness.

Your train of thought may look like this: "That was a great workout I had this morning. While I was exercising, all I thought about was burning calories and building muscle. But you know what? My mind was so clear after the gym this morning that I had so much more energy to —" (fill in the blank with any good deed you may have done). This gives purpose to the workout and realigns it to a holy intention.

And what about the forbidden acts? Those are a lot tougher, nearly impossible, to release from the hands of the *kelipah* (those evil spiritual forces mentioned above). But say that going against the will of G-d makes you feel really disconnected as a Jew, and you sincerely wish you can reconnect to G-d on a very deep level. And say that this disconnection makes you so spiritually thirsty that you reveal a deep yearning to fulfill G-d's *mitzvot* in a more devoted manner than before. After the fact—with such intense, sincere repentance, and with such a deep, deep level of love towards G-d—the sins can turn around and become "merits," for they are responsible for that feeling of desiring to reconnect to G-d on such a high level.

(Inspired by Chapter 7 of Tanya)

 TANYA BIT: It's never too late to reverse an act done "mindlessly," without a G-dly intention.

WHEN GOOD INTENTIONS FALL SHORT

NOT EVERYTHING CAN BE G-DLY

It's a hard one to swallow. You may have all the good intentions in the world and may sincerely wish to make someone happy, but if you go against their express desire, they most definitely won't be pleased. Like the time I wanted to surprise my parents for their anniversary, so I cut up some precious original photos to turn into a collage. I didn't ensure that there were doubles, nor did I ask permission to irreversibly snip their sentimental pictures into the design that I saw fit. Great intentions, but I nevertheless caused some damage.

Imagine you decided to eat a nourishing meal and intended to direct the energy you derive from that meal to concentrate on a stimulating Torah class. But if the food that you are consuming is not of the kosher variety, then even though you had altruistic intentions, it can cause spiritual damage. The nonkosher food becomes part of your flesh and blood, and even if you use the energy derived from it to learn Torah or to have energy to pray, the *kelipot* (evil spiritual forces) have a handle on the food and the energy you get from it.

The same goes for thinking thoughts that are prohibited by the Torah (such as lustful thoughts), speaking words that are prohibited (such as slander), or acting in any manner prohibited by the Torah. Even if you feel justified, these actions are "tied" to the *kelipah* and therefore forbidden to a Jew.

So while you can upgrade a mundane act into a holy one by consciously inserting a good intention (like going shopping to have nice clothing to wear on Shabbat), good intentions don't give you a free "pass" to go against G-d's will. *(Inspired by Chapter 8 of Tanya)*

 TANYA BIT: Serving G-d means doing what He wants on His terms.

THE STRUGGLE IS REAL

CHAPTERS 9—15

Armed with the knowledge that you have two opposing forces inside of you, you begin to tackle your challenges. At the same time, you accept your limitations: you can't eradicate the desires of the animal soul completely. You can rein them in, though, and it is "close to you" to become a *beinoni*, the hero of the Tanya. While you will not attain the level of a *tzaddik*, you can strive to emulate one.

YOUR OPPONENT ... NOT REALLY

THE ANIMAL SOUL'S FACADE

It's a convincing act. Your G-dly soul tries to assert itself over your body, enjoining your thoughts, speech, and actions to express holiness. Your animal soul swoops in like a medieval king fighting for territory, desperately trying to win over those very same thoughts, speech, and actions to its mundane, selfish desires. It's an endless battle, and you are the battlefield.

The animal soul's "base" is in the left chamber of the heart, which is filled with oxygenated blood, and the energy of the animal soul vests itself in the blood as it circulates. The rich blood is symbolic of the animal soul's passion for pleasure and the dominance of its emotions. G-dly soul "headquarters" spreads from the mind to the right side of the heart, the chamber with deoxygenated blood. This used blood symbolizes how the emotions of the G-dly soul are subservient to its intellect.

Your G-dly soul has a strategy. If it can get you thinking about G-d, then you will feel love towards G-d. If those feelings are passionate enough, they can even influence the animal soul to get swept up in the excitement, and it too can develop an appreciation for holiness. The animal soul, however, counteracts with a strategy of its own, distracting you with worldly temptations and lustful desires.

That's where the act comes in. As much effort as the animal soul invests in diverting you from living in a G-dly manner, it really wants to lose. It is like an undercover agent or a coach who is pushing you to strengthen your spiritual muscles, silently begging you to say "No!" to every one of its sinful or selfish suggestions. The truth is that the animal soul is happiest each time the G-dly soul gains the upper hand. So it is your opponent, but not really. *(Inspired by Chapter 9 of Tanya)*

 TANYA BIT: The animal soul tries to tempt you in numerous ways, but it wants you to see through his act.

FUNDAMENTALLY DIFFERENT

THE NATURE OF A *TZADDIK*

There are some people on this planet who don't care which flavor of ice cream they're eating—or if they eat ice cream at all! These people do not indulge in physical pleasure; in fact, they despise it. Their service of G-d is completely altruistic; there isn't even a struggle. Welcome to the world of the *tzaddik*, the righteous person.

This ain't the level of me and you. Instead of a constant battle between good and evil, the *tzaddik* has transformed his animal soul so that it, too, desires G-dliness. The conflict is officially over. Service of G-d consists of how much he loves G-d and, by extension, how much he detests evil.

The incomplete *tzaddik*—of which there are many levels—has accomplished this to various degrees. His love of G-d (and hatred of evil) may be partial. He still has zero expression of the evil of the animal soul in his daily life, but there's a vestige of it still lurking in his heart.

And then, there's the complete *tzaddik*, rare in every generation. A complete *tzaddik* has the highest level of love for G-d; there is no trace of evil left in his animal soul. He does Torah and *mitzvot* without any ulterior motive—not even to satisfy a deep, spiritual craving. He serves G-d for one purpose: G-d's sake alone.

In order for us to understand which level we can strive for, we need to understand our limitations. We will never be a *tzaddik*, because that is a person fundamentally different from the rest of us. What remains is to emulate and learn from a *tzaddik's* behavior, by cultivating our love for G-d and lessening our attachment to physical pleasures, without being disappointed that we will not in fact be rid of our selfish desires so quickly. *(Inspired by Chapter 10 of Tanya)*

 TANYA BIT: The more one loves and appreciates G-dliness, the less one is drawn to indulge in selfish, physical pursuits.

THE ANIMAL SOUL MAY WIN THE BATTLE, BUT NOT THE WAR

THE NATURE OF THE *RASHA*

You could punch it, kick it, ignore it or wrestle with it, but it will never be defeated. This is the personality of the G-dly soul, which never gives up the good fight against the animal soul.

We are now introduced to another category of people: people who sometimes stumble. Their animal soul gets the better of them, and they let down their guard, going against G-d's will temporarily. They give in to lust and temptation; their reason is eclipsed by their emotions. Thanks to their G-dly soul, however, they will regret their actions and ask G-d to forgive them. Sooner or later they may fall again, but they will repeat the cycle of repentance. Welcome to the world of the *rasha*, or the category of "the wicked who are full of remorse."

There's a wide range in the category of *rasha*. There are "the wicked who know good"—people who may sin in thought, speech, or action; and people who will sin in all three categories to various degrees of duration and frequency. Yet even when "the wicked who know good" intentionally (or unintentionally) allow the animal soul to win a battle, the animal soul doesn't win the war. The G-dly soul then pipes up, causing the person to sincerely repent to G-d, who forgives the *rasha*.

Then there is a small percentage of people who have shut down the voice of their G-dly soul so much that they don't even hear it. They may consistently go against G-d's will without a second thought of remorse. They are called "the wicked who know only evil," since they are not even conscious of their G-dly soul. However, even in such a case their G-dly soul is still ever-present, albeit in a distant manner. That is why, regardless of how many sins a Jew has committed, "over every gathering of any 10 Jews rests the *Shechinah*." *(Inspired by Chapter 11 of Tanya)*

 TANYA BIT: The animal soul can temporarily win over the G-dly soul, but the G-dly soul always perseveres.

ROUND-THE-CLOCK RESTRAINT

A WHOLE NEW CATEGORY CALLED THE *BEINONI*

There was a video circulating recently of two teenagers being rude and disrespectful to police officers, filmed and shared by the teens themselves. They mocked, taunted, and jeered at the officers, accusing them of doing nothing on the job and just collecting a paycheck. While the repulsive behavior of said teens made me want to give them a piece of my mind, I was filled with admiration for the policemen. They kept their cool and didn't respond to the kids. They were visibly containing themselves, using every ounce of self-control to maintain their dignity and not lash out at the boys.

We could all use some restraint sometimes. There are times when we are ready to lose it, about to explode in anger at another. There are times when we could be severely tempted to sin when forbidden desires seem to beckon. The animal soul can get dangerously close to getting us to transgress, and yet we don't actually have to act on its desires. Welcome to the world of the *beinoni*, the category in between, who is not free of temptation like the *tzaddik*, nor does he indulge like the *rasha*.

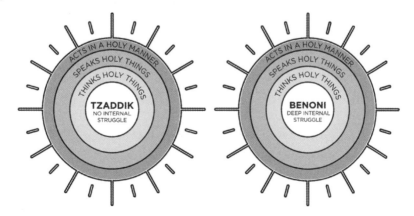

The *beinoni* is synonymous with self-control—a person who does not express anything unG-dly in thought, speech, or action. Very human, he feels the desire to do the wrong thing and the craving for physical satisfaction. But it stops right there. He excels at impulse control, using every ounce of willpower to fight the temptation, diverting his attention to holier pursuits. His behavior looks like a *tzaddik's*, because he is a master at behavioral perfection. Yet inside he struggles mightily not to give into lust and the animal soul's inclinations—whether regarding sins against G-d, such as eating nonkosher food, or sins against man, such as taking revenge. The *beinoni* simply rejects the demands of the animal soul to indulge.

This is the revolutionary concept taught in Chapter 12 of Tanya: You and I have the natural ability to be a *beinoni*. It is not a spiritual ability per se, but a neurological one. My mind can control my heart, and therefore it is my greatest tool to assist me in the battle against the animal soul's emotions and desires.

(Inspired by Chapter 12 of Tanya)

 TANYA BIT: My goal in life is not to be a *tzaddik* but a *beinoni*, exhibiting self-control one situation at a time.

DEFINING "RIGHT SIZE"

WE CAN'T DO IT ALL ON OUR OWN

In an all-too-human fashion, we sometimes find ourselves swinging from feelings of grandiosity to feelings of incompetence. One minute we are G-d's gift to the planet, and the next, encompassed by feelings of insignificance, we are lowly creatures for having base desires.

To clear up both misconceptions, the Tanya helps us become "right-sized" in our minds, understanding that we may never be perfect like a *tzaddik*, but that struggle doesn't define us as evil.

There's something else the Tanya clarifies. On our own, we'd likely fail. Left to our own devices, the animal soul would be extremely powerful, winning many battles against our G-dly soul. The animal soul states its opinion ("it's just a white lie," for example), and the G-dly soul states its opinion ("be honest and truthful"), but a final verdict needs to be issued.

That's where G-d Himself helps us, as our sages say: "Man's evil inclination gathers strength daily.... And if the Almighty did not help him [i.e., help his good inclination], he could not overcome it." Our G-dly soul is granted an extra dose of holiness that serves as a "helper" to encourage the Divine soul to win.

At the same time, in order to suppress feelings of smugness or complacency when we are doing the right thing, we are cautioned to "be in your own eyes like a *rasha*" *(see Chapter 1)*. This doesn't mean to mistakenly think that we are actual sinners, just that we are like them; beneath the surface there is an animal soul lurking, urging us to sin. Yesterday's success does not guarantee today's. However, with G-d's help we overcome its desires, striving at all times for behavioral control.

Does the animal soul ever pipe down? It does. When a *beinoni*—your average Jew who is controlling his thoughts, speech, and action—prays (the Shema and the Amidah) with intense love of G-d, the animal soul "goes to sleep," lying dormant and ceasing its distracting chatter.

But the rest of the day? For most of us, the majority of it is spent managing the homefront, ensuring that the G-dly soul emerges victorious in this world of continuous internal conflict.

(Inspired by Chapter 13 of Tanya)

 TANYA BIT: During prayer, we can experience temporary relief from the desires of our animal soul.

RELATIVE TRUTH

A *BEINONI'S* "RUBRIC" IS DIFFERENT FROM A *TZADDIK'S*

A young boy hands his math test to his dad, with a large red 100 percent.

"I'm disappointed, son," says the father. "You think you truly know your math? Why, I'm sure if you took a test in college-level calculus, you would fail." The son is left feeling bewildered... Of course, no father would say such a thing to a young child. The kid is only being judged on his knowledge of the times table, not on the math that is above his ability.

The same is true with the hero of the Tanya, the *beinoni* (the individual who struggles inwardly but acts perfectly outwardly, not succumbing to his temptations). Unlike a *tzaddik* (the perfectly righteous individual), the *beinoni* cannot muster up a consistent level of love of G-d that will permanently silence the desires of his animal soul. He will constantly struggle, and it will take all his efforts just to maintain behavioral perfection.

However, just because he does not fully succeed in his emotional perfection, that does not render his service of G-d "untrue." Though his love of G-d fluctuates throughout the day, he can consistently access it during prayer. G-d does not expect him to be a *tzaddik*, nor does G-d judge him by a level that is beyond his ability. It is therefore irrelevant that he would not pass at being a *tzaddik*; he is expected to excel at being a *beinoni*. That is his truth.

In the Tabernacle, one middle bolt secured all of the beams from end to end by passing through the middle. This is spiritually symbolic of the fact that just as each beam had its inner core, or truth, every person has a level of Divine service that is authentic for him or her. And it is this level that we need to strive for 100 percent. *(Inspired by Chapter 13 of Tanya)*

 TANYA BIT: G-d expects me to excel, but within the framework of the natural ability He bestowed upon me.

BEST ATTEMPT

MIMICKING THE *TZADDIK*

I must have tried 20 diets as a teenager, but one stands out in my mind.

There was this CD you were supposed to listen to that would help condition you not to eat certain foods. "Don't look at fries as a delicacy!" the voice on the CD bellowed, "but imagine the fat, in a concealed form, clogging your arteries!" Constantly listening to such messages was going to be the key to my weight loss, for how could I contemplate eating something that my brain perceives as being repugnant? The guy might not have been too far off.

In Chapter 14 of Tanya, the author sums up the type of Divine service accessible to every single Jew. This is hinted to in the beginning words of the oath that the soul takes before descending to this world *(see Chapter 1)*:

On the one hand, *Al tehi rasha* ("Don't be a wicked person"). Regardless of how much you want to indulge in a selfish or sinful act, you can choose to abstain by reminding yourself that you don't want to be disconnected from G-d for even one moment.

At the same time, *Tehi tzaddik* ("Be a righteous person"). Even though you will most likely never lose your feelings of pleasure from material things, you can temper them by choosing to meditate on how short-lived self-gratifying pleasures are, and learning to associate them with a feeling of repulsion. You can also make your best attempt at mimicking a *tzaddik* by meditating on the greatness of G-d—on the one hand teaching yourself to appreciate a higher level of pleasure, and on the other, learning to experience spirituality as a "real" pleasure. *(Inspired by Chapter 14 of Tanya)*

 TANYA BIT: While you cannot completely let go of your attraction to material pleasures, you can develop a slight aversion to overindulgence and an appreciation for spirituality.

A SPIRITUAL WORKOUT

YOUR EFFORT MATTERS

I was building up from scratch; I was so out of shape that 10 minutes on
my elliptical was a big deal. But I slowly worked my way up to half an hour,
three times a week, and fell into a routine. One day I felt ready for more.
I braced myself, and when 30 minutes passed, I continued pedaling. "Just
five more minutes," I told myself, yet every turn of the pedal was strenuous,
disproportionately harder than the entire 30-minute workout.
The struggle was real.

It's that way spiritually, too.

The verse *(Malachi 3:18)* says: "And you will return and see the difference between the righteous
man and the wicked one, between the one who serves G-d and the one who does not serve Him."

It's easy to understand the difference between a righteous man and a wicked one. Is the second
half of the phrase merely repetition, saying the same thing in different words?

The Talmud explains that it is not. "The one who does not serve Him" is a Jew who learns
something 100 times, the acceptable standard in the days of the Talmud. "The one who serves
Him" is the Jew who pushes himself to learn the material just one more time—an effort that could
equal the entire previous 100 times.

"The ones who do not serve Him" are the people who are perfect, but it isn't hard for them.
They may even be *beinonim*—perfect in thought, speech, and action. They naturally enjoy learning
Torah, praying, and "being good." They are comfortable in their status quo, and even if they
wanted to act inappropriately, they could easily squelch the desire. They're simply used to it. They
may be "goody-goodies," but that's not called serving G-d.

Then there are "those who serve G-d." This is the individual who pushes himself beyond his comfort zone and has to actively inspire himself in order to "win" over his evil desires. He has to summon deep reservoirs of strength and love of G-d in order to keep his *beinoni* status.

And that is just as hard, if not harder, than everything he's ever done, which makes it worth as much as, or more than, everything he's already accomplished. The hallmark of someone considered to be serving G-d is the fact that he struggles. The moment he serves G-d out of habit, he is a *beinoni* who "does not serve Him."

Because G-d appreciates the effort.

(Inspired by Chapter 15 of Tanya)

 TANYA BIT: A spiritual workout begins where my comfort level ends.

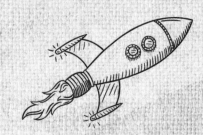

MOTIVATION:
THE LONG WAY
CHAPTERS 16—17

With long-term investment and daily reflections, it is "close to you" to literally create enthusiasm and emotions of love and awe of G-d. You can think your way to these feelings by meditating in detail about G-d's greatness, and even if you are not filled with the greatest passion for G-d, your daily investment will yield enough love and awe to motivate you to serve Him. This method is known as The Long Way, because it takes lengthy and consistent practice to yield results.

A BRAINY EMOTION

YOU DO YOUR PART, AND G-D WILL DO HIS

You follow a recipe to the T, and yet it royally flops. You adhere to the formula faithfully, but somehow it doesn't yield the results you anticipated. Is there something wrong with what you are doing—or worse, with you?

While a failed pastry may reflect on a faulty recipe or on a person who did not follow it exactly, when it comes to following Torah's directives, there is something else at play.

If you follow the Torah's protocol for serving G-d, then even if you don't experience the kind of results you anticipated, you need not feel frustration over not seeing tangible results of your efforts. The results are G-d's department.

Say you are a spiritually hardworking Jew who spends a considerable amount of time meditating about the greatness of G-d in the hopes of creating a deep love and awe of your Creator. You may be successful and feel an intense awe and fiery love of G-d. Your emotions then supplement the act of the mitzvah with spiritual wings, which lift the mitzvah to higher spiritual worlds. *(This will be discussed more in later chapters.)*

However, you may also find, to your surprise, that while you may develop an appreciation for G-d and intellectually understand that you "should" be drumming up a palpable love in your heart, no such love develops. You might be disappointed, but you are not at fault.

In Chapter 16 of Tanya, the Alter Rebbe reassures you that that's OK. Some souls are just not the "type" to be gushing with passionate love for G-d, even after praying and meditating at length. The most they experience is *tevunah*, an intellectual or "brainy" emotion.

If you are such a person, then this *tevunah* suffices as sufficient motivation to perform the *mitzvot* and acts as "wings" to the *mitzvot*, enabling them to rise heavenward, as if motivated by a conscious love.

This is the meaning of what it says in the Talmud, "The Holy One, blessed be He, joins a good thought to the deed." If a Jew has a "good thought"—meaning, invests in meditating about G-d— then even if he or she does not reveal tangible emotions in their heart, G-d allows the *tevunah* to function as if it's a real feeling. And so, He links the "brainy emotion" with the mitzvah it motivates. It is considered like "the real thing."

(Inspired by Chapter 16 of Tanya)

 TANYA BIT: I am responsible for the effort. G-d is responsible for the result.

MOTIVATION TO ACT

WHAT "CLOSE TO YOU" REALLY MEANS

Despite the hefty price tag, many successful companies invest in motivational speakers and workshops to inspire members of the company to work as a team. The expense is necessary because a motivated team maximizes productivity. And productivity is the bottom line in the business world.

The Torah describes serving G-d as follows: "For this thing is very close to you, in your mouth and in your heart, that you may do it."

This seems to be the opposite of human experience. Maybe it is "close" for us to serve G-d with our mouths (by praying or saying words of Torah) or by acting as G-d wants (by doing *mitzvot*). But how is it "close" or accessible for us to serve G-d with our hearts? Isn't it difficult to generate feelings of love and awe of G-d?

Yet the Torah is not demanding that we feel exploding fireworks of passion towards G-d. It's simply telling us to motivate our hearts to want to do the acts commanded by G-d. How? By choosing to think about and focus on G-d's greatness as the Creator of us and of our world. *(In later chapters, the Tanya provides specific meditations to do this.)* This should help us muster the motivation necessary to tear ourselves away from a computer screen or get off the couch to pray—or do whatever G-d wants from us at this moment.

While it's nice to be able to feel totally in love with G-d, if that is not possible, we can at least feel motivated to serve G-d; we "just" have to actively use our brain.

There is one exception to this. When a *rasha* repeatedly gives in to every one of his heart's whims and desires, the system malfunctions. He no longer can control his heart via his brain. He desires something, and he automatically gives into it, without any ability to put on the brakes. How then is it "close to him" to be motivated to serve G-d? He first must repent and shatter the hold that the *kelipah* (negative spiritual forces) have on him. Once he sincerely repents, he, too, can think his way to love and awe of G-d, enough of both to motivate him to fulfill G-d's *mitzvot* and refrain from transgressing.

That's why it says "in your heart," followed by "that you may do it." We're definitely capable of creating a minimal amount of emotion so that we want to do what G-d wants, as well as to keep away from what He doesn't want.

Because in Judaism, action is the bottom line.

(Inspired by Chapter 17 of Tanya)

 TANYA BIT: I can use my mind as a tool to motivate myself to do what G-d wants from me.

MOTIVATION:
THE SHORT WAY
CHAPTERS 18—25

With a short reflection on the following chapters, it is "close to you" to uncover an innate sense of enthusiasm for serving G-d. Should you feel an urge or impulse to do something contrary to G-d's will as expressed in the Torah, you can mentally inspire yourself by revealing your soul's natural love of G-d, or your spiritual adrenaline. While it takes a number of chapters to explain, once you master the technique it is a quick tool to have at your disposal. This method is known as The Short Way.

INNATE FAITH

YOUR SOUL'S WELL OF FAITH

Some people inherit riches, and some people inherit properties. Some businesses are even bequeathed to a number of generations. As a Jew, you have been granted an inheritance as well. It's not a financial one, but a spiritual one. Your soul is spiritually predisposed to something of a spiritual nature—an inborn faith and love of G-d, inherited from your forefathers.

One way of serving G-d with emotions is to contemplate G-dliness, arousing deep and passionate feelings of love and awe, enough to motivate an ardent service of G-d ("the long way"). However, when you are short on headspace or ability, there's another route to revealing love of G-d ("the short way"). This is not by creating a new love of G-d that never existed before, but by revealing a latent love of G-d that resides in the soul of every Jew just because he or she descends from Abraham, Isaac, and Jacob. The Patriarchs were "chariots" to G-d's will, because they inserted as much of their own opinion and ego into their service of G-d as a chariot inserts when being led by a horse: none at all. As a reward for their selfless service of G-d, the forefathers merited that each of their descendants inherited this love, regardless of whether they are observant. The source of this love is in the level of the soul called *chochmah*, which refers to a spark of intellect that is not yet formulated or understood. That's because this love and fear transcends understanding and reason.

Some expressions of this are the examples of Jews throughout history who gave up their lives rather than renounce their faith. They may not have known much about their heritage, but they unknowingly acted on the light vested in their souls in the form of an illogical yet inherent faith in one G-d. *(Inspired by Chapter 18 of Tanya)*

 TANYA BIT: "This thing is very close to you." Love of G-d is very close to you, for it is already in your heart.

ACTIVATING THE SOUL

YOUR SPIRITUAL ADRENALINE

I feel it before every big event. I'm functioning on practically zero sleep, there are a million details to take care of, and somehow, even with all the stress, I feel a surge of energy that keeps me going—an energy that I simply cannot muster up on an average Tuesday. It isn't logical, but my adrenaline is activated.

My soul also has an extra energy that, under specific circumstances, can be turned on and brought to the surface.

What does this extra energy look like? It is the latent love of G-d found in the soul of every Jew. This love also includes awe and fear, the fear of disconnecting from G-d. Just as a flame tends to flicker—as if aiming to return to its core elemental root—the soul of a Jew "flickers," itching to attach itself to its root, to G-d.

So why don't we all feel this super love of G-d? Because our ego gets in the way. And the thicker our sense of self, the dimmer our connection to this light in our soul. That's why this spiritual energy can lie dormant, without an ability to be mobilized.

Until it feels threatened.

When a Jewish soul feels threatened that it will be disconnected from G-d (such as when put to a test of faith with a rallying cry of "Convert or die!"), the spiritual adrenaline is activated. If a flame would successfully separate from its wick, it would actually disappear. So too, a soul which would separate from the body and return to its source would essentially be giving up its life.

But it is willing to do so under such conditions; this is called *mesiras nefesh*, ultimate self-sacrifice. When the soul feels the duress of disconnection ("Convert!"), then even a person who struggled to have access to this latent love of G-d can access it in full measure and break free from the animal soul ("Die!"). Like adrenaline, the reaction is swift, automatic, and powerful.

(Chapter 25 of Tanya will discuss how to access this spiritual adrenaline even without being in a do-or-die scenario. Keep reading.)

(Inspired by Chapter 19 of Tanya)

 TANYA BIT: Lack of humility prevents me from feeling the true desire of my soul, which is to reconnect with my source: G-d.

AFFIRMATION
YOUR SOUL'S DEEPEST DESIRE

We all have those moments as parents. Your kid comes home 15 minutes later than he was told, or doesn't want to get into pajamas. You ask him not to jump in the rain puddles right now, or to eat or not eat a certain food. The child doesn't want to comply, or demands an explanation, and you respond with "Because I said so." There are times when a child needs to learn simple obedience and recognize his parents' authority. Regardless of what the request was, those words encompass it all.

There were two fundamental rules—or commandments—that we heard directly from G-d Himself, as they include in them all the positive and negative commandments in the Torah. "I am the L-rd your G-d" includes all positive *mitzvot*, for by following His will, I am saying that G-d is #MYG-d. I am affirming my belief that there is nothing and no one else other than G-d, and that even my own existence or desires are but nothing compared to Him. I accept the command and G-d himself, because He is the ultimate authority, and He said so. This affirmation is my soul's deepest desire.

"You shall have no other gods" includes not committing any sin, because there is no "other" than G-d; therefore, I do not transgress even one of His commands. This is what my soul wants to avoid.

(Inspired by Chapter 20 of Tanya)

 TANYA BIT: Every mitzvah I do reaffirms my belief in G-d's Oneness, and that there is nothing else besides Him.

CONSTANT CREATION

WHAT YOUR SOUL REALLY WANTS TO AFFIRM

Creation is a fascinating biblical story that took place thousands of years ago, and now the world functions on its own. Sound right? G-d uttered 10 sayings, and poof! The world came into being and has been running independently ever since.

Not quite.

According to the teachings of Kabbalah, the same speech—or revelation of energy—that G-d used to create the world is perpetually repeated in order for the world to remain in existence. In other words, G-d is constantly recreating. Just as a Frisbee can remain airborne only as long as there's lift, creation exists only as long as G-d is "speaking" it into creation.

Understanding the daily story of Genesis is key to understanding G-d's oneness, or what it means that "G-d is everything." Because every single thing is being kept alive by G-d at every single moment, there is no existence independent of Him. While we may not be aware of it, we are united with G-d at all times. G-d designed the world in a way that we cannot tell that it is being spoken continuously into creation, due to its seeming self-sufficiency, yet G-d's unity is still absolute truth.

The unity is even more profound than the metaphor of human speech. For when a human speaks, once the words leave the realm of thought, the words are an entity outside of him- or herself. However, when it comes to G-d's words—and by extension, the entire world—they are still a part of His existence. There is no place devoid of Him. Therefore, G-d's words (and His creations) are contained within Him even *after* he utters them, in the same way a human's words are contained within him *before* he utters them.

Got your brain in knots? That's because G-d's "speech" functions very differently than a human's, and calling G-d's words "speech" is, well, just a figure of speech.

(Inspired by Chapter 21 of Tanya)

 TANYA BIT: I exist only because G-d is recreating me at this very moment.

SUBTLE DENIAL

WHAT YOUR SOUL REALLY WANTS TO AVOID

There are people who think they're G-d. They may not actually think it in those terms, but they are so arrogant that they take full credit for all of their accomplishments, denying that G-d had anything to do with it.

Remember King Pharaoh? He boasted: "The river is mine, and I have made myself!" He denied not G-d's existence, but His oneness. There was G-d, and there was Pharaoh.

Denying G-d's oneness is idol worship. And while G-d created a world where we subjectively seem independent of Him, His intention was that we would invest effort to discover the truth—that at every moment He is our true life force. Imagine a window veiled by layers and layers of curtains. Push aside the curtains—the *kelipah*—and you will reveal the great sunlight. Our job is to see through the thickness of the *kelipah* and acknowledge that it is G-d's light-giving energy to every living thing: and that not only are there no "other gods," there is no "other" existence outside of G-d.

When we forget to give G-d "credit" and swell with conceit at our successes, we worship ourselves, which is a subtle form of denying G-d.

(Inspired by Chapter 22 of Tanya)

 TANYA BIT: Humility is acknowledging G-d's oneness. Arrogance is denying it.

INTERNAL WILL

YOUR SOUL'S DESIRE IS TO FULFILL G-D'S DESIRE

What came first, the chicken or the egg? It's not only a joke, but a deep philosophical question debated by many wise individuals. What was the cause and what was the effect?

In a similar vein, a question is posed: What came first, the creation of the world or G-d's desire for *mitzvot*? Was there a beautiful world that would be perfected by people exhibiting kindness, or did G-d desire kindness—and therefore created people who could be kind to one another?

It's the latter.

G-d had a deep desire. And He created and sustains the entire universe in order for people to fulfill that deep desire: the *mitzvot*.

When you want ice cream, you don't have to consciously direct your feet to the nearest ice-cream store. Your limbs actualize your desire automatically. *Mitzvot* are dubbed "limbs of the king" because they are the actualization of The King's inner will.

And just like a car has no opinion or will of its own, but is a vehicle to fulfill the will of the driver, so too when Jews do a mitzvah they are completely selfless, fulfilling the reason they were created. That is why the Patriarchs were called "chariots" *(see chapter 18)*: at every moment of every day, they were concerned only with fulfilling G-d's will, riding through life with the subservience of a chariot to its rider.

(Inspired by Chapter 23 of Tanya)

 TANYA BIT: When I use my hands to give charity, they become a chariot, or vehicle, for G-d's innermost will.

INTIMATE KNOWLEDGE

YOUR SOUL'S DESIRE TO BE INTIMATE WITH G-D

When a random stranger does a favor for you, you probably feel grateful. It's so nice that someone went out of their way for you—that he or she was highly considerate when not even knowing you.

But that's the thing: they don't even know you. As kind or friendly as they are, there is a distance between you and them. There is no closeness, attachment or familiarity. They don't know the deepest parts of you, what makes you tick. There's no intimacy.

When you learn the words of Torah, there is intimacy. You're not "just doing G-d a favor" by fulfilling his *mitzvot*; you are getting to know G-d. Instead of merely fulfilling His will with your actions, your garments of thought and speech are becoming one with it (assuming that you are learning and also verbalizing the words of Torah). Since halachic rulings constitute what He likes and represent His truest desires, engaging your mind at a Torah class is uniting your soul with G-d's will *(see Chapter 5)*, which is one with G-d Himself.

There's more that learning Torah accomplishes. While G-d is constantly "aware" of His unity with His creations, creations aren't. *(See Chapter 21.)* There's a gap in perception, and Torah learning bridges that gap. It reveals a deep and G-dly light, and exposes the truth of reality—that G-d and His people are united in an inexplicable, inseparable manner.

With true intimacy.

(Inspired by Chapter 23 of Tanya)

 TANYA BIT: Learning Torah is getting to know G-d himself.

OUT OF TOUCH

THE HEAVY PRICE OF DISREGARDING YOUR SOUL

Everyone's got a pet peeve. You know, those things that get on your nerves, whether logical or not. Imagine a good friend who is very aware of what sets you off, but goes ahead and deliberately does that very "thing" that you just can't stand: not a great strategy to promote connection.

That's one way to understand what it's like when a Jew engages in one of the 365 prohibitions in the Torah. With G-d, it's not a petty annoyance, but going against the very purpose of why He created the world! Whether it is a "small sin" or a "big sin" is irrelevant; the fact that G-d doesn't like it causes a disconnect between Jew and G-d. It represents denial of G-d's will, and a momentary decision to disconnect from G-d. In fact, a sin renders a person even lower than *kelipah*! Because while *kelipah* is merely as an agent for G-d to tempt man, engaged in negativity at G-d's instruction (and still hoping man will triumph over it), a sinner is directly disregarding G-d's commands.

It's not always a conscious decision. On the words "If a man's wife turns aside [and commits adultery]," the sages comment that the Hebrew word for "turns aside" (*sisteh*) shares a root with the Hebrew word for "folly" (*shtus*). An adultress has lapsed not only in behavior but in judgment. The spirit of "folly" convinced her that a sin does not really cause any disconnection from G-d, and she bought into that lie.

She didn't consciously ignore her soul's desire to connect to G-d and fulfill all His wishes. She didn't consciously drag her soul through the mud as she went against an express law in the Torah. She was simply out of touch with the truth. Just like she would never sever her connection to G-d by converting from Judaism, she would never want to sin and do something that is not in line with G-d's will, temporarily pulling the plug on the relationship.

To avoid sinning, she would have to free herself from the spell of the spirit of "folly."

Because at the core, every Jew wants to be one with G-d.

(Inspired by Chapter 24 of Tanya)

 TANYA BIT: Being conscious of my soul prevents me from unconsciously disconnecting from G-d.

PLEDGE OF ALLEGIANCE
HOW TO REMAIN CONSCIOUS OF YOUR SOUL AND ACCESS YOUR SPIRITUAL ADRENALINE

A Russian peasant was once bragging to his friends about his allegiance to the czar. "If I could, I would give my life up for the czar! If I had gold and silver and riches, I would give my entire fortune to the czar! Anything I own I would happily donate for the greater cause of the czar and my country!"

His friend Ivan replied: "And your two chickens that you actually own, would you give those to the czar?!" Suddenly the Russian peasant wasn't so sure…

It's all about translating the theoretical into the practical.

In this chapter, the Tanya wraps up "the short way" to accessing a preexisting love and fear of G-d, tying together all the pieces from chapters 18–25:

A Jew, under threat, would rather give up his life than his connection to G-d *(Chapter 19)*. But the power in this is not only his willingness to die when circumstances actually warrant it, but to use that willingness to arouse his natural, but sometimes dormant, love and awe of G-d *(Chapter 18)* in day-to-day living.

It is feasible for every Jew.

The very premise of the book of Tanya is that it "is very near to you" to have a palpable love and fear of G-d. How? When a Jew becomes conscious that there is nothing else but G-d, and that every mitzvah unites him with that reality *(Chapter 23)*—and every sin disconnects him from it *(Chapter 24)*—it becomes blatantly obvious which choice he wants to make. When he further realizes that, from a certain perspective, every prohibition is similar to bowing down to an idol, that activates his spiritual adrenaline and latent love of G-d, which absolutely won't tolerate the thought of disconnection and will go to all lengths to prevent the sin.

There is a central "pledge of allegiance" that Jews recite twice daily to serve as a reminder. In the Shema prayer, a Jew says, "You shall love the L-rd your G-d with all your heart, with all your soul, and with all your might." This means loving G-d to the point of self-sacrifice.

The meaning of the Shema prayer message is as follows: "If I theoretically would be willing to surrender my very life for G-d's sake, I can practically choose to get in touch with my soul's true desire and surrender any temptations that are not in line with G-d's Torah, as well as overcome any laziness in performing positive *mitzvot*. Rather than connecting to my Source by leaving my body, I will connect the flame of my soul with its source by living in line with G-d's will."

And do it out of love.

(Inspired by Chapter 25 of Tanya)

 TANYA BIT: Reciting the Shema can release my "spiritual adrenaline" and reveal the love and fear of G-d that I naturally have.

STATE OF JOY

CHAPTERS 26—34

Who are "you"? Are you a body or a soul? The more you identify as the latter, the more you will be able to feel a sustainable and long-lasting happiness. In addition, the more you relate to your own G-dly soul, the more you will improve your ability to relate to the G-dly soul in fellow Jews, thus improving your interpersonal relationships. The Tanya helps troubleshoot some of the more common obstacles to joy, and teaches us how to target guilt, shame, and apathy.

READJUSTING PRIORITIES

HOW TO HANDLE IT WHEN THE CHIPS ARE DOWN

Sometimes, life happens. You're walking down the street with your new iPhone and drop it, only to find the glass cracked, resembling a spider's web. Or, after many loyal years on the job, the new boss fires you. Or you simply don't feel like you have energy to get out of bed in the morning.

These things don't affect only your mood. When you are down, your defenses are down as well. And that affects your entire ability to manage your spiritual battlefront, making it easy to fall prey to the desires and temptations of the evil inclination.

So how do you conquer this?

In Chapter 26 of Tanya, the Alter Rebbe lays the foundation for how to overcome depression over real physical challenges. The premise is that a good G-d does only good, but sometimes that manifests as "revealed good" (what we like), and sometimes it manifests as "hidden good" (what we don't like). While "hidden good" appears negative or uncomfortable, it actually stems from a higher spiritual level, allowing a person to grow and feel a closeness to G-d that is unattainable through "revealed good."

If a person operates only on a material level, then it is devastating to receive a perceived blow. However, one who is in tune with their spirituality can readjust their priorities and accept that even though this is not the reality they would have asked for, it can be used as a springboard to connect to G-d on a higher level. Since "The Most High abides in secrecy," a deeper connection to G-d is more available when individuals are presented with challenges; they can appreciate this as more meaningful than physical pleasures, as in the verse *(Psalms 63:4)*: "For Your lovingkindness [a relationship with G-d] is better than life [physical good]."

It is for this reason that those who can be happy despite their problems are called "lovers of G-d" and will receive a similar reward in the world to come, in the form of a more open revelation of G-dliness.

(Inspired by Chapter 26 of Tanya)

 TANYA BIT: When a curveball is thrown your way, it can either disrupt your life or enhance your life. The difference is in your priorities and your perspective.

EXPOSE THE GUILT

IT IS NOT GOOD FOR YOUR SOUL

Does Judaism endorse guilt trips? It sounds so self-righteous to feel really bad about committing a sin, thinking about it all day to the exclusion of all else.

In fact, it's downright dysfunctional. Even worse, it's counterproductive.

It becomes a vicious cycle. If at work or throughout the day you are focused on your mistakes and defects, then you are bound to feel down about them. Which makes you susceptible to tripping and indulging even more in the very things you are trying to avoid.

So how should you deal with depression over spiritual downfalls? By exposing the guilt for what it is—a clever ploy of the evil inclination to make you battle-weary and more likely to give in to lust and temptation.

There is a healthy alternative to dealing with your mistakes: setting aside intentional time in the evening, not while at work or play, to review your behavior. With a clear mind, you can make an honest reckoning of where you need to make improvements. You can then rest assured that G-d forgives you completely ... and move on.

(Inspired by Chapter 26 of Tanya)

 TANYA BIT: Rather than obsessing over the past, strategize for the future, ensuring that it is productive and not destructive.

SHAMELESS STRUGGLE

DON'T LET STRUGGLE DEMORALIZE YOU

Do you find that there were certain things that challenged you many years ago, and feel despondent that 5, 10, or 20 years later you are still up against the same internal struggles?

Does it bother you that while you consider yourself a moral and spiritual person, you still find yourself at home or work tempted by desires to speak or act in a manner that you are ashamed of?

You are not alone.

The nature of the human condition is to struggle. Instead of feeling downhearted that yet again you are tempted by your senses, you can feel joy, for only when you battle temptation can you fulfill an actual mitzvah in the Torah: "You shall not follow after your heart and after your eyes, by which you go astray."

These words weren't commanded to saints, but to the *beinoni*, the term coined to describe your average human. For reasons known only to G-d, He experiences tremendous pleasure every time you squelch a negative desire.

There is no shame in struggle. If anything, shame is rooted in a person's ego, where he expects himself to be exempt from the struggle experienced by the rest of humanity. And while this may come as a surprise to some, our very purpose in this world is to wrestle with our compulsions and impulses, trying time and again to subdue and tame our inner demons.

Here's the incredible part: Every time you don't give in to a negative desire, you weaken its power over you. And that automatically weakens the power of negative energy in the world, so that each time you emerge victorious, you lessen the darkness in this world and make the struggle a bit easier for you and everyone else. This is not something a *tzaddik* can do, for he does not battle with *kelipah*. Only a *beinoni*, by rejecting the *kelipah*, can weaken it for himself and for the world around him.

Ever had sweet 'n' sour chicken nuggets? Both "sweet" and "sour" are tasty, but they are very different flavors. The *tzaddik's* service is like a "sweet flavor" to G-d, and the *beinoni's* service is like a "sour flavor." They are both tasty to G-d, and He desires that each serve Him with their respective abilities.

So by not acting out on a negative impulse, you flavor the world in a way that only a *beinoni* can.

(Inspired by Chapter 27 of Tanya)

 TANYA BIT: Internal conflict is not a letdown, but a reason to rejoice.

STIFF COMPETITION

IT MEANS YOU'RE DOING SOMETHING RIGHT

You're feeling on top of your game, motivated. You want to do things right, and you idealistically make the time, bright and early in the morning, to learn or pray. But just as you are all set, your mind is flooded with torrents of distracting thoughts, from the mundane to the downright forbidden.

Can't your brain ever give you a break? Can you ever have peace from the pesky animal soul?

Not really. Even if you do experience a reprieve, it is only temporary.

Rather than feeling down about undesirable thoughts, you should be glad, because if your animal soul is putting in effort to distract you, it signals that it's in trouble. Just as a big business won't reckon with a company unless the CEO perceives it as actual competition, the animal soul wouldn't try so hard to pull you away if you weren't involved in something good.

It's not that you're a hypocrite. There are two forces trying to corner the market and get the lion's share of your brain. Your animal soul gets so nervous while you are learning or praying that it desperately makes an attempt to counteract these positive actions.

If it felt like it had the upper hand over the G-dly soul, it would likely rest on its laurels. If it's picking up speed in the form of inappropriate thoughts or desires, then it means that you're doing well.

So, how should you deal with it?

Simply ignore it. Don't get busy engaging with negative thoughts or figuring out how to deal with them. Wrestling with temptation is like wrestling with a dirty man: you are bound to get dirty from the interaction. Instead of focusing on how to respond to the temptation, or what *not* to think about, throw your energy into what you *do* want to think about. That is the only way to avoid being sucked into the animal soul's whirlpool.

And if you're finding it really, really difficult, then humbly ask G-d to have compassion on you and help you out with your battle against your animal soul.

So that you can go on and pray in peace.

(Inspired by Chapter 28 of Tanya)

 TANYA BIT: When inappropriate thoughts enter your mind at a furious pace, they signal that there is stiff competition. Keep up the good work!

REALITY CHECK

THE ANTIDOTE TO APATHY

What happens if you just don't care? What if, no matter how many chapters of Tanya you learn, you feel apathetic and lack the emotional connection to prayer? Or to personal self-improvement?

It's as if the pipes between your mind and heart are clogged, numbing your feelings and leaving you feeling cold towards anything spiritual.

The Alter Rebbe proposes a radical solution—one that should be used sparingly and only when necessary. For it is a bitter pill to swallow.

The apathy is caused by the arrogance of the animal soul, and the only way to break through it is to humble it. Just as tinder and smaller branches will catch fire faster than a very thick log, the ego may need to be "splintered" in order to kindle a spiritual fire.

A reality check will do the job of thawing the ice.

It is humbling to consider that we humans are capable of lusting after things that are forbidden and contrary to G-d's will. It is humbling to consider past sins, even ones that we have repented for. It can even be humbling to recall the content of dreams that we have experienced.

This process of intentional humbling deflates the ego and disempowers it from blocking our spiritual endeavors. These thoughts actually bring us to a deeper level of repentance and returning to G-d and may even be the reason G-d caused us to feel apathy in the first place: so that we can get to work lighting a richer spiritual fire. *(Inspired by Chapter 29 of Tanya)*

 TANYA BIT: Our feelings of apathy are G-d's way of inviting us to a deeper level of repentance.

RIGHTEOUS INDIGNATION

CALL THE ANIMAL SOUL'S BLUFF

You want to feel warm, passionate, and motivated.

Instead, you remain indifferent and unenthusiastic, plugging along with a
lukewarm Judaism.

You might give off the impression of being smug and perfectly content with the
way things are, but deep down you know that it's really just your animal soul.
And the good news is, there is a way to put it in its place.

You see, the animal soul is a total coward. It projects confidence and ego but retreats to the corner as soon as someone calls its bluff. A well-targeted dose of righteous indignation aimed at your animal soul is the way to call that out.

This additional strategy that the Alter Rebbe proposes to melt through layers of apathy is to rage in your mind against the animal soul, and demand in a stormy inner voice: "Why do you keep getting in my way, making it so difficult for me to serve G-d? Why do you deliberately twist the truth and cause me to stumble?"

The evil inclination of the animal soul has no real substance. Just as darkness disappears as soon as a beam of light appears, the apathy of the animal soul melts away as soon as the light of truth shines.

G-d, too, used the rage method.

When the Jews in the desert doubted G-d's ability to bring them to the Holy Land upon hearing the disparaging report of the spies, G-d grew angry with them, and the Jews did an immediate about-face. Their G-dly soul believed in G-d's ability all along, and really didn't need any convincing. G-d's rage pierced through the arrogance of the animal soul, and as soon the animal soul was put in its place, all that remained was the natural faith that every Jew possesses.

So if your animal soul is ever stubbornly apathetic, directing some good old-fashioned healthy rage right at it will cause its power to vanish.

(Inspired by Chapter 29 of Tanya)

 TANYA BIT: Show some righteous indignation towards your animal soul, and it will stop being a force to reckon with.

A SLICE OF HUMBLE PIE

HUMILITY CUTS THROUGH APATHY

Two guys were sitting in a room, determined to become humble at all costs. They sat there for days and contemplated their lowliness, convincing themselves that they were total nobodies, and truly pious and humble. Suddenly a third guy entered the room and started pacing, mumbling to himself, "I'm a nothing. A nobody. Simple and humble."

The other two nudged each other and laughed. "This guy just showed up, and already he thinks he's a nobody!"

Humility isn't about thinking you are more humble than everyone else. But it is about being more humble than literally every other person on the planet, as our sages instruct: "Be lowly of spirit before every man." How can you appreciate that others, even sinners, are greater than you? By being in awe of their struggles. And by asking yourself if you exert the same inner stamina as they do to combat your own challenges.

It's a definite ego puncture, and sometimes a necessary one. If you find yourself feeling too smug in your service of G-d, you may just need to remind yourself that you're not really that great after all.

Maybe your friend lives or works in a place that is full of temptation? Maybe his or her nature is more passionate than yours, making him or her more susceptible to sin? Do you know the extent of your friend's private demons? Do you have any idea how much it takes to battle such strenuous inner turmoil? And here's the punchline: if Divine Providence had granted you those very same conditions, would you fare any better?

When you think in those terms, you stop thinking you are holier than thou. You start questioning whether you invest enough energy to stop yourself from repeating a juicy piece of gossip or whether you are scrupulously honest in money matters as you should be. You wonder if you make it a regular practice to get out of your comfort zone enough to increase in Torah learning and prayer.

It occurs to you that if you're lucky enough to be well-versed in Torah, then you should be living life on a higher plane: instead of pointing fingers at others, you should hold up a mirror to your own actions and check your own standards. And you realize that you are no better than anyone else, and if anything, may even be lacking in the effort department.

A humbling thought indeed.

(Inspired by Chapter 30 of Tanya)

 TANYA BIT: Sometimes, in order to be truly spiritual, you need to feed your ego a slice of introspective humble pie.

HAPPY FOR YOUR SOUL

THE MIND SHIFT YOU NEED TO HAVE

It's the domino effect of medicine. You take pills for one ailment, but it has side effects that cause another medical problem. Now you have a new challenge on your hands and need meds to counter that...

In order to combat the spiritual ailment of apathy, the Alter Rebbe advised serious stocktaking to pierce through the arrogance of the animal soul. But what happens if that leaves you feeling depressed? Even though you carefully applied the above advice with the appropriate dosage, now you may have a new problem on your hands.

The Alter Rebbe explains how it is not really a problem. If soul-searching causes you to feel temporarily depressed, then channel it into motivation to do better. Instead of wallowing in *atzvut* ("depression"), redirect that energy into *merirut*—a "bitterness" that will motivate you to do more for the good of your soul. Depression is self-centered and drains you of energy. Bitterness is soul-centered and motivates you to right your wrongs. Channel the self-pity into self-growth, and when you reveal the light of your G-dly soul, it's like freeing your soul from the imprisonment of the animal soul.

Meaning: Instead of feeling down by how materialistic your body's desires are, be joyful that your soul is completely unaffected by it, and put all your energy into making your soul happy.

If you use the negative emotions in this manner, this becomes an engine to make your soul happier than it would have been without your down moments. Your renewed sense of commitment to your soul is all by G-d's design, that there should be *yeridah letzorech aliyah*—a low that will propel your soul to greater heights.

The good news is that every time you fulfill your soul's desire to do *mitzvot*, you elevate the animal soul as well.

If your soul is deliriously happy that you are recommitted to doing what she really desires, can you be happy for your soul?

(Inspired by Chapter 31 of Tanya)

 TANYA BIT: My animal soul might trip me up, but my G-dly soul remains untouchable. Isn't that a reason to rejoice?

THE HEART OF TORAH

THE RIPPLE EFFECT OF THE MIND SHIFT

Imagine you were put on the spot with the following request: "Can you please teach me the entire Torah on one foot?"

Torah is vast. Torah is deep. There are thousands and thousands of volumes of books expounding on the Torah. Try capturing it in a one-liner!

The Talmud relates that Hillel the Elder was asked exactly that, and here was his response: "The mitzvah of *ahavat Yisrael* [loving your fellow Jew] is the entire Torah, and the rest is commentary."

What is "Torah on one foot"? Torah is about prioritizing soul over body and learning how to see beyond the external trappings of the world. If you can absorb Torah's message and relate to your soul as a real entity, then you can relate to the soul of another Jew and have true *ahavat Yisrael*.

On a body (physical) level, we are separate people with many differences and opinions. There is competition, jealousy, getting under the skin. But on a soul (spiritual) level, we are literally brothers and sisters, as all our souls come from one loving father, G-d Himself.

Not by coincidence, this chapter in Tanya is Chapter 32, the numerical equivalent of the Hebrew word *lev*, meaning "heart." The heart of Tanya and the heart of Torah are one and the same: to love all Jews unconditionally, by seeing beyond what separates us and tuning in to what unites us.

What about Jews you hesitate to love due to a perceived lack of observance? Does the Talmud not teach *(Talmud, Pesachim 113b)* that "If you see your friend sinning, it's a mitzvah to show contempt towards him"?

The specifics are important. In order to qualify as "your friend," the sinner needs to be on the exact same spiritual level as you, and they need to be close enough to be able to accept rebuke from you. Such a person you should rebuke, albeit lovingly. (When it comes to anyone else—and that is the majority of people—draw them in with thick cords of love, and bring them closer to Torah.) But still, how can you reconcile the mitzvah to love your friend with the Talmud's instruction to hate him?

The truth is, it is not a contradiction. You are displaying loathing for their sinful behavior, not for their essence. You can show them love for their *soul*, while simultaneously showing contempt for their *behavior*.

And there's a way around it. Rather than a love/hate relationship, you can show them compassion. This is hinted to in the verse "Jacob who redeemed Abraham." Jacob is the prototype of compassion, and Abraham the prototype of love. When you feel sorry for someone who is sinning, and have compassion that their G-dly soul is exiled in the grips of their animal soul, you can neutralize any negative feeling of contempt and turn it into a genuine feeling of love for their pure soul. In that way Jacob (compassion) redeems Abraham (love), and allows only positive emotions to fill your heart.

For we are all one people.

(Inspired by Chapter 32 of Tanya)

 TANYA BIT: If I am a body and you are a body, then your existence interferes with mine. But if I am a soul and you are a soul, then we are only one existence.

THE SECRET TO REAL HAPPINESS

BOOKMARK THIS CHAPTER!

It seems that everyone is searching for happiness these days. Check out the self-help section in the bookstore, and the studies shared all over the internet. Observe the extensive and sometimes futile chase on which people embark in the elusive pursuit of that far-off goal.

When done properly, however, it can be a holy pursuit.

The Alter Rebbe suggests the following meditation: Spend time contemplating G-d's absolute oneness, how He is found everywhere and is constantly recreating you. The world only has an *illusion* of independence; in truth, everything is really G-dliness. Think about the existence of a flame, and how if it would be placed in the sun, it would be absorbed into the sun and cease to exist independently (of the sun). Recognize that we are like the flame absorbed by the sun, Jews absorbed by G-dliness.

Allow yourself to feel that no matter where you are, you are infinitely close to an infinite G-d. Think about the fact that when you are actually thinking these thoughts, your brain is acting as a humble abode to G-d, and your soul is fulfilling the very purpose for which it was created— to reveal G-d's oneness here in this world. What greater joy can there be than a deep sense of fulfillment that you are doing what you were created to do?

In fact, that is the reason we recite daily in our prayers: "We are lucky! How good is our portion! How pleasant is our lot! How beautiful is our heritage...." The secret of G-d's unity was inherited by all Jews, and the ability to access true joy is open to us all.

And the joy is a double one. In addition to feeling your soul's joy as a result of your faith, aren't you happy for G-d that His vision is being acted upon: that the raison d'être for creating this universe is being fulfilled at this very moment by you, His beloved creation? Your *emunah*, your faith, will spur you to fulfill as many *mitzvot* of the Torah as you possibly can. And G-d's truest joy is when darkness is transformed into light as a result of the *mitzvot* we perform in the physical world.

And we get to be a part of that.

If you are searching for material pleasures, the chase will be endless, for it is never enough. If you are pursuing a spiritual joy, then true happiness is indeed attainable.

(Inspired by Chapter 33 of Tanya)

Note: The Lubavitcher Rebbe taught 12 Torah passages (*pesukim*) to children that incorporate the most basic tenets of Judaism and include within them the tools to serve G-d. It is fascinating that two of the 12 passages are found in Chapter 33 of Tanya, underscoring how crucial it is for children to be imbued with a sense of mission and taught the secret to lasting joy.

 TANYA BIT: Fulfilling my purpose brings a double joy: my soul's mission is accomplished, and G-d's desire is satisfied.

WHERE IS G-D?

THE JOY OF BEING A MINI-TEMPLE

How long is your attention span? How long can you concentrate deeply on the unity of G-d, meditating on His greatness? If you're like most people, you have your limits. And when you've reached your capacity, it gets too strenuous.

So, what is one to do?

Historically, Jews reached their capacity too. At Mount Sinai, G-d revealed Himself to the Jews, and it was so intense that their souls couldn't handle it. Therefore G-d commanded them to build a Tabernacle, and then a Temple, to (so to speak) "contain" G-d. Granted, G-d is everywhere, but G-d still gave them a place where He would be openly revealed, and they would be able to access G-dliness in that manner.

So where does that leave us today? The Temple is no longer here, and we have limited intellectual abilities. How can we access G-d during the rest of our waking hours?

By learning the laws of the Torah.

Today there are no revelations at Mount Sinai and no majestic structure to behold G-d's greatness. But when a Jew learns Torah, he is learning G-d's wisdom and making it a part of himself. In this way he literally becomes a temple for G-d, containing and accessing G-d's wisdom while in exile. Even if one has time for only learning one (or part of one) chapter of the Torah in the morning and one chapter at night, he can succeed in his quest to "host" G-d in his very own brain, especially keeping in mind that when he does have more time, he will indeed spend it studying more than his regular share.

And when we don't have time to study the laws of Torah? We can still be a temple for G-d by mimicking Him. G-d is good, and G-d is a giver. By giving charity generously, we can elevate all of our time and working hours, making them vehicles for revealing G-dliness in this world.

(When your life revolves around making a temple for G-d, you will be filled with the deepest satisfaction and joy possible. However, that doesn't mean you will be free of negative emotions. Your heart can handle two opposite emotions simultaneously, such as joy because of your G-dly soul and bitterness due to the ego of your animal soul. *See Chapter 31.*)

So go ahead and make your soul happy—and host G-d in your very own Temple!

(Inspired by Chapter 34 of Tanya)

 TANYA BIT: Where is G-d? Wherever you reveal Him.

THE BOTTOM LINE

CHAPTERS 35—38

Regardless of what you feel like when you perform a mitzvah, fulfilling the mitzvah is the bottom line. Each mitzvah has a cumulative effect that will ultimately bring about the final Redemption.

WHAT'S THE POINT?

HOW *MITZVOT* REVEAL G-D'S LIGHT

I was working out on the treadmill, and my son was looking at me strangely. "But what's the point, Mommy?" he asked. "Why are you walking if you're not even going anywhere?"

It was clearly his first time watching me. "Walking is the point, sweetheart! My goal isn't to get to a specific location, but to burn calories."

The protagonist of the Tanya, the *beinoni*, has a similar question: What is the point of all the effort he invests in serving G-d if he sees no actual improvement? He may fill his days with good deeds, but he still struggles constantly with his evil inclination and will never be a *tzaddik*. It seems like he's going nowhere!

Except that is exactly the point. Not to reach a destination per se, but to burn spiritual calories.

The Zohar cites an analogy illustrating this idea. In order for a flame to burn, a wick is not enough; it needs oil to burn as a long-lasting candle. The Zohar compares the *Shechinah*, G-d's revelation, to a flame, and the human body to a wick. In order for the *Shechinah* to be revealed in a person, it needs fuel to keep it burning.

That's where those spiritual calories come in. Doing physical *mitzvot* provides fuel for the flame of the *Shechinah*, and the only way to reveal G-d's *Shechinah* is by physically performing a mitzvah.

Why are *mitzvot* like fuel? Just as physical fuel gets completely consumed as it becomes light and loses its identity, doing a mitzvah is a way to create G-d's light, as there remains no conscious existence. If all I have are emotions for G-d, then I am consciously feeling my own existence.

There's a me that is feeling the love, and G-d's presence cannot be revealed when the sense of self is so thick. But when I do a mitzvah, it's about G-d, not about me.

In other words, selflessness is the key to revealing G-d's light, and doing a mitzvah for G-d is exactly that. So while I may not be transforming my animal soul completely to the same extent as a Tzaddik, I am harnessing its energy as an active participant in revealing holiness in the world.

(Inspired by Chapter 35 of Tanya)

 TANYA BIT: The *mitzvot* are G-d's inner will and the point of it all.

HOME SWEET HOME

MAKING G-D FEEL AT HOME IN THIS WORLD

Imagine coming home after a long day at work only to find your home invaded by strangers, sprawled out on your couch after raiding your pantry. They barely glance at you when you enter, and when they do, they squint and wonder, "Who are you? Do you think you own this place?"

G-d had this inexplicable craving when He created the world in which we live and all the spiritual worlds. And the craving had to do with the former. Through a process known as *hishtalshelut*, G-d created a chain-like descent of spiritual worlds, from the highest spiritual world to the lowest physical world. The "higher" the world, the more revealed G-dliness; the "lower" the world, the more curtains there are on G-d's light. It is on this physical planet that G-dliness is hidden, as nature seems to operate independent of G-d. *(See Chapters 22, 23.)* The world is an illusion that hides G-d's constant re-creation, with forces outright denying that He is the owner of this house.

His *taavah*? He wanted people to see through it. He wanted to be acknowledged as the true owner and Creator. Not by angels or spiritual beings in "higher" spiritual worlds, but by physical people who live in this world of confusion. Every time a Jew performs a mitzvah, he or she tears down a bit of the *kelipah*, the forces that deny G-d.

G-d gets immeasurable pleasure when a mitzvah is performed, and His deep desire to feel "at home" in this world is fulfilled. The world had a taste of G-d feeling "at home" when He revealed Himself on Mount Sinai. And ultimately, G-d is awaiting the messianic era, when the whole world will acknowledge Him, and His great light will shine throughout His entire home on this earth.

(Inspired by Chapter 36 of Tanya)

 TANYA BIT: Every mitzvah is fulfilling G-d's desire of designing a comfortable home for G-d on planet Earth.

YOUR PIECE OF THE WORLD

THE CUMULATIVE EFFECT OF YOUR MITZVAH

Some projects take a lot of work. Say you're stitching a giant needlepoint with a huge variety of colors and intricate details. It takes hours and hours to complete such a masterpiece, needing plenty of patience to go along with it. But when you are finished, there's an inherent reward. It's not something external, like an ice cream cone; your reward is intrinsic. It's the needlepoint itself, ready to grace a wall in your home.

Mitzvot work in much the same manner. When a Jew does a mitzvah, he or she elevates a chunk of the world. For example, if Jews perform the mitzvah of shaking a *lulav* and *etrog* during Sukkot, they elevate those ritual items and draw down a holy light upon them. The energy that people use to do the mitzvah also becomes holy, and that is why the more energy invested in a mitzvah, the more holiness is drawn down.

Not only that, but all the food that that person ate—providing the energy to do the mitzvah in the first place—gets elevated as well because it indirectly assisted in the performance of the mitzvah. In this way, with every good deed performed, more and more of the energy in the world becomes transformed. Thus, the reward is not something external; it becomes the cumulative effect of the mitzvah itself. The reward is intrinsic—a world transformed into a holy place, otherwise known as the messianic era.

Here's the important part. No one can transform the corner of the world reserved just for you. Every soul was put on this earth for one purpose: to elevate sparks assigned to that particular soul. This makes every Jew indispensable in the global endeavor of drawing down holiness into the world.

Not all *mitzvot* are equal. Some require more effort and sacrifice, such as giving tzedakah. When people donate hard-earned money to a cause or charity, they pass up on things that would enhance their own lives. The more effort and energy a mitzvah requires, the more of the world it transforms. It is more effective in completing the worldwide "project" of elevating this physical, mundane world into a holy home for G-d and completing the purpose of creation.

(Inspired by Chapter 37 of Tanya)

 TANYA BIT: There is a little piece of the world that is waiting for you, and every jew, to make it holy.

CALLING G-D OVER

WHY TORAH LEARNING IS IRRESISTIBLE TO G-D

It's hard to have to interrupt yourself.

Imagine you are deeply concentrating on a Torah thought, learning and focusing on the subject at hand, and your mother phones to ask you for a favor. Should you stop? You're finally in the thick of a good explanation on a deep aspect of Torah…

If no one else can fulfill the mitzvah, the sages teach that it is up to you to do so. Because "the most important thing is not study, but practical observance."

That being said, what if your mother doesn't need you, and your sister happily offers to do the favor instead? If the action is taken care of by someone else, is there any advantage to continuing your learning of Torah?

In the remainder of Chapter 37, the Alter Rebbe balances out his emphasis on physical *mitzvot* by underscoring that Torah learning is important as well and, in certain aspects, is even greater than fulfilling an actual mitzvah.

What aspects?

In terms of changing the world, doing a mitzvah is more effective. But in terms of changing your *inner* world, the world of your thoughts and your speech—and the entire intellectual capacity of your soul—Torah is more effective. While *mitzvot* are compared to G-d's limbs, Torah is G-d's wisdom, and permeating your intellect with G-d's is transformative.

There's also something irresistible to G-d about Torah learning. It's like when young children endearingly call out to their moms and dads; parents can't help but melt and respond. Learning Torah is like calling G-d over, and He can't help but respond.

So while *mitzvot* are needed to fulfill the purpose of creation, learning Torah is crucial to our personal growth and relationship with G-d.

(Inspired by Chapter 37 of Tanya)

 TANYA BIT: Learning Torah is inviting G-d into our lives, and "G-d is close to those who call to Him."

MOVE YOUR LIPS

TRUE SPIRITUALITY IS EXPRESSED IN PHYSICALITY

There are times when your soul craves to be spiritual, and there are locations
that seem so conducive to filling that need: a retreat in the mountains, a walk at
sunset on the beach, a guided meditation deep in the woods. But while doing
so can feel very spiritual—and you may even experience a closeness to G-d—it
remains a subjective experience until you move your lips, actually uttering words
of prayer to connect to your Creator.

It's not enough to believe that G-d is one; it is crucial to pronounce it out loud by reciting the
Shema. It's not enough to be grateful to G-d for sustaining you; it is crucial to acknowledge it by
saying Grace after Meals. That's because your soul up in Heaven already knew the truth about
G-d! Its entire purpose in descending to this world is to have the body in which it resides echo the
same truth, by reciting words of Torah and prayer aloud.

It's easy to get carried away in the loftiness of mind and place. But the purpose of creation is to
remain grounded in this earth, using your physical body and energy to do actual *mitzvot*, and to
pray to G-d, enunciating every word.

So go ahead. Move your lips.

(Inspired by Chapter 38 of Tanya)

 TANYA BIT: Judaism is not about disconnecting from the physical to reach the
Divine, but bringing the Divine into the physical.

PASSION

CHAPTERS 38—40

While action is the bottom line, feeling passion for doing a mitzvah has significance. Love and awe of G-d are like wings for a mitzvah, causing them to "take flight." While *mitzvot* fulfill the purpose of creation, emotions illuminate them.

G-d desired not just a home, but a *lichtige dirah*—an illuminated home. *Mitzvot* permeated with passion bind together to create a dwelling place for G-d.

ARE YOU FEELIN' IT?

ADDING "SOUL" TO YOUR MITZVAH

Ever go out with a friend to a restaurant, eager to try out new tastes and foods, only to find the chef's special to be called "Grandma's cream of mushroom soup"? Or to see at the bottom of the menu "a taste of home"?

What are they trying to mimic? Not the actual measurements and spices. They are attempting to evoke a sense of nostalgia, of the loving memory of grandmothers everywhere stirring and serving large pots of soup. That's because beyond the chopping and the peeling, humans crave to feel the passion and intention that comes with a sense of home.

After spending a number of chapters highlighting the importance of just fulfilling the physical requirements of a mitzvah, Chapter 38 presents us with the flip side. Sure, we can do *mitzvot* like a robot, checking them off mindlessly. But G-d craves that we do them with intention, known as *kavanah*. The same G-d who wants us to perform a mitzvah, such as eating matzah on Passover or waving the *etrog* and *lulav* during Sukkot, wants us to do so with the intention of connecting to Him! He wants the experience to be filled with passion, which gives life to the mitzvah. Our sages compared a mitzvah without *kavanah* to a body without a soul, for it is the emotions that give soul to the mitzvah. When a mitzvah is performed with the express intention of connecting to G-d, it literally contains a greater quantity of G-dly light.

There are actually varying levels of doing *mitzvot*, ranging from a "robotic" performance to the "human" performance of them, each one symbolized by a higher form of creation:

1. *Domem* (inanimate object): A physical act done without any emotion at all is compared to an inanimate object, one that exists but is not in any sense "alive." This is the lowest level.

2. *Tzome'ach* (plant): Some physical *mitzvot* inherently involve some thought on the part of the person performing it—such as prayer. Yet if they are done without passion, they can be symbolized by a plant, which experiences growth and is more "alive" than an inanimate rock.

3. *Chai* (animal): When a person does a mitzvah motivated by a natural love of G-d, it can be likened to an animal, which is very much "alive," but operates only on a natural, instinctual level.

4. *Medaber* (human): And when a mitzvah is performed with a love and fear that is intellectually stimulated, it represents the ultimate level, where we are inserting that "human touch" and "taste of home" into the mitzvah itself.

So while the first thing is to make sure that you are actually going through the motions, don't stop there! The next step is to ask yourself if you're really feelin' it.

Because passion will illuminate your mitzvah.

(Inspired by Chapter 38 of Tanya)

 TANYA BIT: Doing a mitzvah with the intention of connecting to G-d not only enhances our mitzvah; it is the way G-d wants us to serve Him.

HIGHER THAN THE ANGELS

YOUR *MITZVOT* CAN RISE TO THE CHAMBERS OF THE RIGHTEOUS

A Chassid once took out his prayerbook to begin praying, folding the corner
of one specific page before he began. Another man in the synagogue noticed
that the Chassid's siddur had many such fold marks, as if folding the corner of
one page was a daily occurrence. The Chassid explained, "My concentration is
limited, and I struggle to focus on the entire morning prayers. But if I fold over
one page, then when I reach that point in prayer I can ensure that—for at least
one prayer a day—I am fully present and concentrating."

Chapter 39 of Tanya may very well be the source for his actions. The Alter Rebbe discusses the
spiritual address of a mitzvah performed or a prayer uttered. What happens to a mitzvah, or a
prayer, once it is performed or recited? If recited with the proper intention, the mitzvah or prayer
rises up to G-d's heavenly chambers, where it merges with the spiritual lights (*sefirot*) found there,
ultimately uniting with G-d's unlimited light (*Ein Sof*). It thus comes "before G-d."

While no GPS can pinpoint their location, there are four spiritual worlds (*see Chapter 36*), or
chambers. The first is *Atzilus*, where G-d's unity is apparent. Each subsequent world is less spiritual
(which means it has less revealed G-dliness) than the one preceding it. The second world is *Beriah*,
the world of intellect. The third is *Yetzirah*, the world of emotions. And finally *Asiyah*, the physical
world of action.

The world where the angels reside is called *Yetzirah*, the world of G-dly emotion, where angels
serve G-d out of love and fear. However, *Yetzirah* is a lower-level chamber, because angels serve
G-d only out of instinct, worshipping G-d in a fixed emotional state. They are stagnant and have
no free will. The world where the souls of righteous people reside, *Beriah*, is greater in its spiritual
nature, for it is the world of G-dly intellect, because righteous people serve G-d not by instinct, but
by using their intellect to create a love and fear of G-d.

When a Jew performs a mitzvah or prays with an instinctive, inherent love and fear of G-d, the mitzvah rises and merges with the G-dly lights (*sefirot*) of *Yetzirah*. But when a Jew contemplates G-d's greatness and feels a love or awe of G-d as a result of his or her intellectual effort, the resulting mitzvah rises to the higher world of *Beriah*, merging with the G-dly lights of *Beriah*, the home of the righteous. That is because a mitzvah motivated by an intellectually generated love and fear of G-d has a superior quality to it, which makes it rise to a world that is higher than the angels.

What about if a mitzvah is performed with no intention at all, but simply out of habit? Or if someone got so carried away during prayer that instead of thinking of love and fear of G-d, they are completely distracted by mundane and unrelated thoughts? Or even worse, if they did it with self-serving motives in mind?

If you cannot muster up the energy to pray with proper *kavanah* (intent), go ahead and pray anyway, because you will one day come to pray with intent. Keep on doing the deed, for one day the feelings will come.

Additionally, one can always repent. While *mitzvot* and prayer without intention cannot rise and merge with those great G-dly lights, one can do repentance after the fact, or reinsert an intention into past prayers, releasing those good deeds and prayers to their appropriate spiritual destination.

This means that one Shema prayer recited with concentration and devotion, arousing intellectually generated awe and fear of G-d in the heart of the Jew, can cause the Shema prayers of an entire year to rise together to the world of *Beriah*, to the world which is higher than the angels.

(Inspired by Chapter 39 of Tanya)

 TANYA BIT: If yesterday my mind wandered during prayer, today I can concentrate and cause two prayers to soar to the high spiritual worlds.

SOARING HIGH

LOVE AND AWE MAKE YOUR *MITZVOT* FLY

They're furry. They're yellow. They make adorable little chirping sounds. Baby chicks are the most perfect little things, except for one thing: They don't yet fly. They're just not mature enough.

When a mitzvah is performed in its entirety, but is lacking motivation and feeling, it is compared to a chick that cannot fly. It may fulfill all the requirements, but it cannot soar and unite with G-d as it could when it is permeated with emotion, with *kavanah*.

The two emotions of love and fear are like wings that lift the mitzvah to reach its fullest potential. Just as a kosher bird that is missing its wings is still technically kosher (but sorely missing a key component of its being a "bird"), a mitzvah done without motivation is technically kosher and still a mitzvah, yet missing an essential ingredient of being one.

Why is *kavanah* so crucial to a mitzvah? Because a mitzvah itself is a very physical activity, done with very mundane items. Physicality operates under an illusion that it has its own existence, and G-d is not readily apparent on planet Earth. Since *mitzvot* are done with physical objects that by their very nature disguise G-dliness, in order for the mitzvah to pierce through the illusion and rise heavenward it needs a spiritual boost. The spiritual nature of *kavanah*, and the emotional and mental effort involved, serves as the spiritual engine that propels a mitzvah to be able to rise and unite with G-d.

This doesn't imply that one should pursue spiritual passion as an end in itself. That would be similar to a thirsty person who looks longingly at a cool glass of water without taking a sip to quench his thirst. The whole point of spirituality is to arouse an intense love and longing for G-d, which can be quenched only by actually drinking His Torah and doing His *mitzvot*.

When you have the "body" of the mitzvah combined with its "soul," the mitzvah has reached maturity.

(Inspired by Chapter 40 of Tanya)

TANYA BIT: A "mature" mitzvah is one that is fulfilled with passion, allowing it to soar heavenward and unite with G-d.

HOW TO FEEL

CHAPTERS 41—50

Experiencing love and awe of G-d is not only for deep spiritual seekers, but it is "close to you," whoever you are. In the following chapters the Tanya teaches various meditations that, when practiced, will actually cause you to feel levels of love and awe of G-d.

SOMEBODY'S WATCHING

THE FOUNDATION OF OUR RELATIONSHIP WITH G-D

"Dance as if nobody's watching," the saying goes. Let loose, be yourself, and move without a care in the world.

Is that a good thing? There's a certain amount of self-respect that allows for healthy inhibition, the decency to act appropriately when someone is watching.

The truth is, there is always somebody watching. And that somebody is an all-knowing, all-encompassing Being: G-d Himself.

That awareness is actually the basis of a relationship with G-d and the necessary foundation for avoiding negative commandments, as well as fulfilling positive ones.

When I contemplate for even a few moments that the great and awesome G-d wants to have a relationship with me—and is perpetually "standing over me," aware and interested that I serve Him properly—then I am bound to be filled with awe in my heart, or at least in my mind. When I meditate on the details of creation, from the Seven Wonders of the World to the miracle of a newborn life, from the crashing waves of the ocean to the budding of a flower, and appreciate that G-d fills and transcends all of it, I feel a self-consciousness that I am being watched: a G-d consciousness.

Love of G-d, while a vital ingredient in my relationship with Him, cannot serve as the foundation for it. Love feels good, and therefore has a selfish component. In order to transcend my own desires and be willing to put G-d's will before my own, I need to access a basic level of awe of G-d that will prevent me from rebelling against Him.

The great sage Rabbi Yochanan ben Zakkai blessed his students on his deathbed: "May it be G-d's will that you fear Heaven as much as you fear humans."

Because when we know that someone is around, we are on our best behavior.

(Inspired by Chapter 41 of Tanya)

 TANYA BIT: Pray as if somebody is watching, for that is the basis of serving G-d.

TREASURE HUNT

THE AWE IS ALREADY THERE FOR DIGGING

Companies invest millions into mining for gold or digging for diamonds and other precious stones, often not knowing exactly where they will be found. They simply estimate the general vicinity.

Imagine knowing with certainty that a treasure exists within you, and all you've got to do is dig, dig, dig.

That's how the verse refers to the innate reverence of G-d found within every Jew, waiting to be revealed: "If you seek it like silver and search for it like a buried treasure, then will you understand the reverence of G-d."

As a Jew, you have the capacity to have this fear, or reverence, for G-d, which is enough to motivate you to fulfill His commands. But you have to do the digging.

That means work of the mind. It entails focusing on G-d's greatness and constant presence with fixed concentration (known as *daas*) to the point where it is real to the mind's eye. It takes meditating at length for the awareness of G-d to translate from an intellectual consciousness to an actual feeling. And just like physical digging, it's no easy task.

That's why we get assistance in the following ways:

1) Every Jew has a little spark of Moses's soul in their soul. It is that spark inside us that boosts our ability to have *daas*.

2) Just like every person has a spark of Moses, every generation collectively has a Moses of the generation. Jews get support in the form of soul powers from the contemporary sages and leaders (the souls of Moses) of every era. By connecting to them and learning their teachings, the "digging" becomes easier.

The goal is to feel enough awe of Heaven to refrain from violating G-d's will. As it says in the Torah, G-d asks "only that you revere the L-rd, your G-d, [in order to] go in his ways."

If you spend some time dedicated to this practice in the morning, then at any point during the day that temptation calls your name, you can easily recall the feeling of awe that comes along with the awareness of G-d's greatness.

Because you can always claim your treasure.

(Inspired by Chapter 42 of Tanya)

 TANYA BIT: "Digging" for fear of Heaven is bound to yield results.

AN ARTISAN OF FAITH

ALL YOU NEED IS TRAINING

When I see a pile of grapes on the table, I don't just see grapes on the table. I see dark and light, shadows and highlights, colors and reflections. As an artist, I tend to notice all the details automatically, even if I'm not in the midst of a painting. My eye is trained.

The Hebrew word for faith, or belief, is *emunah*. However, *emunah* is not just about believing, but about practicing to feel the belief. The word shares a root with the word *uman*, "artisan"—a worker in a skilled trade. Just as a skilled worker trains for many years in order to excel at his craft, we need to train our minds to think and meditate on topics that will help us feel a palpable awe of G-d. And just as one would tremble before a king, not because of the pomp and splendor that one sees in the palace but because of the essence of what a king is, we can train ourselves to feel a tangible fear not because of anything specific in the universe, but because of G-d's essence behind it all.

The main thing is to meditate consistently. When we spend time daily contemplating the greatness of G-d, then we'll look around at His world and not just see a world. We will see His awesomeness, His Power, and the fact that He gives life to all of creation. We will see that "the skies, the earth, and all their numerous components" are energized by G-d Himself. We will remember that He wants to have a relationship with us, and that He cares that we do as He asks in the Torah. And we will constantly be aware of His presence.[1]

After all, our minds will be trained. *(Inspired by Chapter 42 of Tanya)*

---

[1] If for whatever reason we cannot actually feel the reverence of G-d, we can rely on generally accepting G-d's authority, as we demonstrate by bowing in the Amidah prayer.

 TANYA BIT: I can train myself to feel awe of G-d by observing the world around me.

ABOUT THOSE PREREQUISITES...

AWE AND LOVE COME IN STAGES

Learning at the uppermost levels necessitates a regimen. Going to law school requires prerequisites. There are mandatory courses to take prior to medical school, and even prerequisites for nursing school.

College courses have prerequisites because before taking a high-level class, students need to be prepared. This ensures that students have a foundation of knowledge and experience in order to advance to more complex concepts.

Torah and *mitzvot* have some basic prerequisites as well. There is typically a hierarchy of emotions when it comes to fulfilling Torah and *mitzvot*, and you can't skip levels, because one builds on the other.

1. "Lower-level" — Reverence and awe of G-d

The sages say, "If there is no reverence, there is no wisdom." In order to access the wisdom of Torah and *mitzvot*, there is a prerequisite: you must have a basic level of reverence for G-d. *(See Chapters 41, 42.)* It is an easier and lower level of fear and reverence, but nevertheless crucial in order to serve G-d properly. It is when you feel so in awe of G-d that you wouldn't dare disobey Him. It is the feeling that emerges from meditating on G-d's presence in both the physical and spiritual worlds, followed by actually performing the *mitzvot*.

2. "Lower-level" — Love of G-d

Fulfilling Torah and *mitzvot* is a prerequisite; only then can you climb the ladder and experience love of G-d. This level is called *ahavat olam*, or "worldly love." It is a love acquired from transferring your love of material pleasures to a love of spiritual pleasures. Naturally, you are wired to love physical pleasures. But rather than loving ice cream, you can train yourself to love the Creator of ice cream by recognizing that compared to G-d, something like ice cream has no value.

Since this food is dependent on G-d for its existence, it is transient, as opposed to G-d, Who is real and everlasting. Who or what is more deserving of your love? Once you comprehend that G-d is the true source of all physical pleasures—and therefore much greater than them—you can shift your love from the worldly to the infinite.

3. "Higher-level" — Reverence and awe of G-d

The sages also say, "If there is no wisdom, there is no reverence." Learning Torah wisdom and observing *mitzvot* is a prerequisite to the higher level of reverence, which isn't about G-d's powers and abilities, but about G-d Himself. Not only is it a prerequisite, but it directly creates the higher-level fear. A lower-level reverence can be compared to the fear of a king—which is essentially a fear based on externalities, the king's might and power. The more powerful the king, the greater is the fear. On the other hand, this higher level is similar to the feeling of embarrassment and sense of abnegation when in the presence of true greatness. At this level you lose your sense of self completely. You are not just in awe of G-d; you suspend your ego entirely. It's not about abstaining from acting out on your desires for the sake of G-d; you simply don't feel your desires! You stop feeling like a separate identity from G-d and instead feel like you are truly one with Him.

4. "Higher-level" — Love of G-d

The higher level of reverence is a prerequisite for an intense love of G-d, where a person does not allow physicality to hide G-d from him. This level is known as *ahavah rabbah*, "great love." This type of passionate love of G-d is a foretaste of the world to come. However, this love is not accessible to all. It is granted as a gift from G-d to a select few, who have succeeded in "climbing the ranks" of the previous levels, reaching an emotional maturity and perfecting their service of G-d.

For the rest of us, the main thing is to keep climbing.

(Inspired by Chapter 43 of Tanya)

 TANYA BIT: Awe of G-d is a prerequisite to serving G-d; however, it is just the foundation.

THE LOVE OF YOUR LIFE

LOVE OF G-D IS SO VERY CLOSE TO YOU

If you were to find yourself in a near life-and-death situation, such as being stuck in the desert without water or lying gravely ill in the hospital, petty things would fall to the side. All that would matter would be your will to keep living. When you sense your own mortality, all you desperately desire is to survive—to have the energy to make it through one more day.

That's because the greatest love of your life is life itself.

When it comes to loving G-d, it can sound intimidating. Can you really come to love G-d, or is that a lofty goal relevant only to the few "spiritual souls" out there?

In Chapter 44 of Tanya the Alter Rebbe explains that you can. On your level, based on your abilities, you can reveal within yourself a real loving connection with your Creator.

Think about it. If your life were in danger, then you would cling to it at all costs, because you already love your life. That's one step over from loving the Giver of Life: G-d Himself!

When you meditate on the fact that G-d is truly the source of your life, you will be filled with love of G-d, as the Zohar explains on the verse "My soul, I have desired you at night; in the morning my spirit longs for you."

Just as the body loves its soul, its very life, a Jew can reveal his or her innate love of G-d. Because G-d is the true love of your life.

(Inspired by Chapter 44 of Tanya)

 TANYA BIT: You already love your life, but you can think your way to loving the Giver of life.

FOR G-D'S SAKE

LOVING G-D LIKE A CHILD TO HIS FATHER

"What are you going to give me if I listen?"

Sometimes kids want prizes for their behavior, or to be acknowledged for their help.

"Mommy, are you thirsty? Can I get you a drink of water?"

And sometimes kids are not focused on themselves, but on their parents. Anything that they can do to make a parent's life easier makes them happy. Children have a natural love for their parent that makes such selfless love possible—to the extent that a child is even capable of giving up his life for a parent.

Every Jew inherited such a love of G-d from the Patriarchs. Meditating about the fact that G-d is our loving Father awakens this natural love and gives us the ability to do His *mitzvot* not for any reward we might get, but because it's what G-d wants. This completely turns the tables from thinking about what we want to accomplish to focusing on what G-d wants accomplished.

It may take some getting used to. A simple tool to get accustomed to this way of thinking is to frequently say out loud: "G-d is my loving Father, and I would do anything to make Him happy."

From our mouth to our heart, we can then serve G-d for G-d's sake.

(Inspired by Chapter 44 of Tanya)

 TANYA BIT: G-d is "thirsty" for my *mitzvot*, and I do them out of love for Him.

GO FOR THE GOLD

A MORE PASSIONATE KIND OF LOVE

All metals were not created equal. Silver might be shiny, copper may look rich,
but none compare to the value and luster of pure gold. So go for the gold.

When you learn about various forms of meditation and the subsequent forms of love for G-d you might experience, you may wonder: If you can easily meditate your way to revealing an inherent natural love (such as loving G-d for giving you life, or loving G-d as a Father),[1] then why work hard to meditate at length about G-d's greatness in order to create a new love of G-d?

Revealing feelings that already exist beneath the surface is a shortcut. It's quick, and gives you the fuzzy feeling of being close to G-d.

But don't forget to also go for the gold, by meditating in detail and with focus on G-d's greatness. In this way, you can feel a new love that is not dependent on preexisting feelings.

The love that is developed "from scratch" through deep intellectual effort—not relying on inherent feelings—is a more fiery and passionate one. In the process of understanding and learning about G-d, and embedding this love within, you are fulfilling the purpose of your creation, as is written in *Raaya Meheimna*: "Man exists in order to know the glory of G-d."

So go for the gold. *(Inspired by Chapter 44 of Tanya)*

---

[1] It should be noted that both these forms of love are a hybrid of higher and lower levels of love: They have an inherent element that is a gift from G-d (higher level love) and they have an intellectually stimulated element that comes with brain work (lower level love.) However, since they both depend on preexisting loves they do not have the quality that *ahavat olam* has, of contemplating your way to a new and passionate love of G-d.

 TANYA BIT: Generate a love of G-d, rather than just relying on a preexisting one, and feel the fire within.

HAVE SOME COMPASSION

ANOTHER ROUTE TO LOVE

He looks angry. He's hanging out with the wrong crowd. He's dressing and speaking in a manner that is beneath him, dragged by his friends into dangerous behaviors. And your heart goes out to this poor lost soul.

When love won't work, compassion will. There are times when you can't muster up the feeling of love for G-d, but you can feel compassion for the spark of G-d inside you, dragged by the animal soul as it engages in behaviors that are beneath it. Just as when you tug at the bottom of a rope, the top of the rope gets pulled as well; when the animal soul is "pulled" into temptations, the G-dly soul is dragged along. And your heart goes out to your G-dly soul, sparking a desire in you to connect to G-d.

This is the deeper meaning behind the verse *(Isaiah 55:7)* "And let him return to G-d, and He will have compassion for him." It's not just that G-d will have compassion for him; he will have compassion for G-d! And when a Jew shows compassion for the piece of G-d inside him, he will be motivated to return to G-d.

Learning Torah and doing *mitzvot* are forms of being "intimate" with G-d. Doing *mitzvot*, especially charity, is like "hugging" G-d; learning Torah is like "kissing" Him. In order to achieve that deep connection to G-d, we have to have some compassion for our soul. This is another application *(see Chapter 32)* of the verse "Jacob [who symbolizes compassion] redeemed Abraham [who symbolizes love]." When love is hard to come by, compassion saves the day.

(Inspired by Chapter 45 of Tanya)

 TANYA BIT: When you feel bad for your soul, you'll be motivated to drag it back out of the mud by connecting to G-d.

RECIPROCAL LOVE

A TWO-WAY RELATIONSHIP WITH G-D

Suppose you received a hand-delivered invitation to have lunch with the U.S. president and first lady, complete with an escort to transport you to the White House. As you dine with the most powerful couple in the land, wouldn't you respond to their warmth with positive feelings of your own? That's the way it is in relationships. When one party initiates gestures that demonstrate love, the other party responds with similar feelings. "Just as water reflects a face, so too the heart of one person reflects the heart of another…"

This dynamic exists in our relationship with G-d as well. When we think of all the good deeds G-d has done for us, we are bound to feel love back towards Him. Consider the following: G-d is an all-powerful being, and yet He has personally done great kindnesses for us as a collective nation, such as redeeming us from slavery in Egypt. He "hand-delivered" an invitation to the Jewish people (to the exclusion of angels!) to spend time with Him, and connect to Him through Torah and *mitzvot*, which He revealed to us on Mount Sinai.

The intimate relationship we forge with G-d through mitzvah observance is compared to the loving, intimate relationship between spouses. That's why before performing a mitzvah, we say: "Blessed are you, G-d … Who has sanctified us with His *mitzvot*," using the same terminology (sanctification) as a husband uses when marrying his wife.

When we meditate on the above, especially during the Shema prayers, it is so very attainable to feel a real and passionate love for G-d.

Because our feelings reflect His. *(Inspired by Chapter 46 of Tanya)*

 TANYA BIT: G-d loves humble little me, and I mirror that with love towards Him.

DAILY ESCAPE

LOVING G-D FOR REDEEMING US FROM OURSELVES

Sometimes we feel like prisoners in our own bodies. It's almost as if we're hijacked by a force that compels us to act in a certain way, perpetuating a bad habit or acting against our own principles.

We can experience a daily escape. When we feel like our body is imposing a limitation on us—not allowing us to be free of its desires (think food, money, power, etc.)—there is a special prayer that can assist us. When a Jew recites the Shema prayer consciously, he says "The L-rd is our G-d, the L-rd is one." When we desire G-dliness, He becomes "ours," so to speak.

When we "own" G-d—when we tap into the fact that He is our own G-d—it empowers our G-dly soul to be free from the desires and compulsions of the body. This is miraculous and similar to the Exodus the Jews experienced from Egypt.

The Hebrew word for Egypt is Mitzrayim, which shares the root of the Hebrew word *meitzar*, "limitation." The "great escape" from Egypt did not just occur once to our people, thousands of years ago, but continues to occur daily in our lives when we recite the Shema and get relief from our personal "Egypts." This is the reason that our sages instituted that directly following the Shema we recall the Exodus—to remind us that this prayer is the key to our personal freedom.

How can we not love G-d for giving us this opportunity?.

(Inspired by Chapter 47 of Tanya)

 TANYA BIT: The story of the Exodus can be my daily story when I concentrate on the meaning of the Shema prayer.

REMOVING THE BARRIERS

REFLECTING G-D'S LOVE BACK TO HIM

You've witnessed the loving scene before. A devoted grandfather wants to interact with his 2-year-old grandson, so he crouches down and meets him eye to eye. He may be a professor, a doctor, or a lawyer, but he avoids any professional jargon and instead speaks simply, on the child's level, pointing at the tot's toy.

"Orange truck?"

And the child smiles and repeats: "Orange truck."

It may take effort on the grandfather's part, but were he to deliver a college-level lecture to the child, it would be way above his head. In order to connect, he needs to remove all barriers.

G-d created a world, and He desired to have a relationship with us. Were He to appear in this world in all His infinite glory, we would not be able to withstand His great light. So G-d "contracted" his light in a process called *tzimtzum*, which means there is only as much G-dly light in this world, giving it life, as we can handle. We exist only because of G-d's diluted light, or energy, that He grants us. But it is done in a manner that does not overwhelm us, allowing us to connect to Him.

The blessings we recite before the Shema prayer help us focus on this fact. The first blessing describes the many angels in their formations, and how completely overwhelmed they are by G-d's infinite light. And yet G-d chose to contract Himself not for the angels' sake, but for ours. They cannot access a close relationship through Torah and *mitzvot*, but we can.

The second blessing describes how much G-d loves us. That's why he "contracted" His great light in order to create a world where we can have a relationship with the Almighty G-d, by observing His Torah. The blessing continues with "And you chose us from every people and tongue ... to give thanks to You...."

When we grasp that G-d "crouches down to us," so to speak, in order to relate to us, we reflect His act of love with a declaration of our own in the Shema by saying, with feeling, "You shall love the L-rd your G-d with all your heart."

A relationship with no barriers.

(Inspired by Chapters 48 and 49 of Tanya)

 TANYA BIT: G-d extends himself to have a relationship with me. How can I extend myself to have a relationship with Him?

CHANNEL THE PASSION

LOVE TRANSLATES INTO ACTION

Music can play games with your emotions. In a single song you can be lifted
to the greatest heights of joy, only to tumble as the lyrics or melody tug at your
heartstrings, evoking deep nostalgia or even pain.

The Levites in the Temple were masters of music so intense that it induced opposite emotions simultaneously, known as *ratzo v'shov* ("running and returning"). Their holy service of creating music was symbolic of the delicate dance between yearning for spirituality ("running") yet channeling the passion into doing a physical mitzvah ("returning").

First comes the "running." You learn about G-d, and you meditate about how "in His presence, everything is considered nothing." You see through the facade of this physical world, and you want to be free from all the dishonesty and selfishness surrounding you. Your soul is on fire with love of G-d,[1] and you relate oh so well to the verse in Psalms, "My soul thirsts for you."

But what should you do with the passion? What should you do with your desire to be spiritual?

Channel all that inspiration back into a pragmatic action, like giving a coin to charity. You're taking all that fiery enthusiasm and, instead of escaping the world, making a U-turn right back into it.

---

1 The love described here is of a different sort than was described in previous chapters. The previous levels of love have a "water quality" to them, as they flow naturally in the direction of serving G-d. This love has a "fire quality," which makes a person want to seek G-d like a fire seeks its source, disconnected from the body/wick. A person has to consciously redirect this love into service of G-d.

This stage is known as "returning," when you channel the passion into doing actual physical *mitzvot*. This is why the Mishnah states: "Against your will, you live." Your soul may prefer to be free from this world and expire, but G-d wants it to remain here and serve Him with the beautiful world He created.

But then you may get too comfortable. As you go about your day, tending to practical "to do" lists, you may forget your fire. The Mishnah reminds you: "Against your will, you die." It implies freedom from the constraints of the body. When you have lost interest and desire in spirituality, it's time to transcend your body again and begin to meditate about G-d, allowing your soul to go for a "run."

Just don't forget to channel your passion.

(Inspired by Chapter 50 of Tanya)

 TANYA BIT: Life is a cycle of creating inspiration and then directing it towards action.

THE LIGHT

CHAPTERS 51—53

Your urges and struggles are not liabilities, but opportunities to withstand the
temptations and reveal G-dly light on this planet.

WHERE IS G-D'S "BRAIN"?

THE GREATEST LIGHT IS IN THE TORAH

"Up, up, down, down, right, left and all around; here, there and everywhere, that's where He can be found!"

These are the lyrics to a children's song describing where G-d is. But if G-d can be found everywhere, what makes a synagogue holy? Was G-d "more" in the Temple, or is He found "more" in my synagogue than in my bedroom?

"From my flesh I shall perceive G-d." This verse in Job *(19:26)* alludes to the fact that many phenomena that take place in the human body are actually a reflection of, and can be used as an analogy to understand, abstract concepts about G-d.

Such as the answer to the above question:

Where is the soul found in a person? On an essential level, the soul is found equally throughout a person's body. The essence of the soul is found just as much in the foot as in the brain. However, on a revealed level, the brain functions as the "control center" of the body, and there is a greater expression of the soul in the brain than in any other part of the body. The soul's energy is expressed primarily in the brain, and from there the eye gets energy to see, the ear to hear, etc.

Similarly, on an essential level, G-d's light is found equally in every part of the world, both physical and spiritual. However, on a revealed level, G-d's light is found primarily in His "brain," the Torah, which is G-d's wisdom. G-d's light can be more expressed in certain locations, such as in the Temple, or today, when "even if one person sits and studies Torah, the *Shechinah* [the term used to describe that G-d is "resting" or "revealed"] is with him." G-d is giving energy and life to everything on this planet, but when a Jew learns Torah, he or she draws down a more overt and powerful revelation of G-dly light.

So the song got it right: G-d is everywhere.

Still, it could probably use more lyrics about how the Torah is where all that energy is most manifest.

(Inspired by Chapters 51, 52, and 53 of Tanya)

 TANYA BIT: Just as the brain is the greatest expression of the soul in a person's body, "distributing" its energy to all the other limbs, the Torah is G-d's greatest expression on earth and is our source of life.

BURN THE HABIT

AND WATCH HOW IT LIGHTS UP THE WORLD!

As children, a bonfire was a full-day activity. First we had to go to the forest around our Upstate bungalow colony and carefully collect the wood and twigs needed to keep a fire going. Only after many hours of collecting—once we had an impressive pile to show for ourselves—could we start the fire. And as we roasted those marshmallows, we knew that the flames would last only as long as there would be wood to burn.

There's a spiritual fire that also needs some "wood" to burn. "The L-rd your G-d is a consuming fire" *(Deuteronomy 4:24)*. Just as fire can catch on to an object only when that object is being consumed by it, so too regarding the light of the *Shechinah*.

In order for G-dly light to illuminate the Jew's soul, the fire must have something to burn—in this case, the negative tendencies of the animal soul. All of a person's arrogance, gluttony, anger, and any other unbecoming characteristic can get burned into holiness.

But how does it work?

In Chapter 35 of Tanya, the Alter Rebbe compared the *Shechinah* to a flame and good deeds to oil. In this parting chapter, the Alter Rebbe repeats this metaphor and highlights a recurring theme of Tanya: Don't despair that you may have the very human desire to cheat, to eat forbidden foods, or even to be promiscuous. For in order for G-d's fire to burn, it needs a "wick" to hold on to, and by "burning" your negative impulses, by fighting them one desire at a time, your base desires become the wick that causes the G-dly glow to shine brightly on this planet.

So embrace each desire of your animal soul as an opportunity to provide "burning material" for G-dly light, and watch this world become a brighter place.

(Inspired by Chapter 53 of Tanya)

 TANYA BIT: Saying goodbye to a bad habit is saying hello to G-dly light.

ACKNOWLEDGMENTS

It is with a great sense of humility and gratitude that I sit down to write my list of acknowledgments. I am endlessly grateful to Hashem for giving me the ability to learn and express my passion through writing, so that I and my dear readers can become close to Him.

I am grateful to Mrs. Chana Weisberg and the team at Chabad.org for accepting my written work and editing it for publication online. I am grateful to Rabbi Yehuda Shurpin for his rabbinic review.

This work would not come into fruition as a book without the dedication of the entire Meaningful Life Center team. I am grateful to Rabbi Simon Jacobson for accepting and spearheading the printing of my manuscript. I am grateful to Rashi Marcus for being an efficient Project Manager and a pleasure to work with. I am grateful to Alex Heppenheimer for his careful editing and to Batsheva Lubin for her fabulous design.

I am grateful to my parents, who raised me with a "can do" attitude and gave me the confidence to embark on creative projects, and to my mother-in-law for her careful edits and feedback. I am grateful to my family and friends who cheered me on, believed in my project, and supported me until the end. And I am grateful to my husband, Rabbi Mendel Blau, who helped me with his unending wisdom and technical help. He encourages me to keep writing and to fill my life with my passions.